Commodore 64
Computing

Commodore 64 Computing

Ian Sinclair

GRANADA
London Toronto Sydney New York

Granada Technical Books
Granada Publishing Ltd
8 Grafton Street, London W1X 3LA

First published in Great Britain by
Granada Publishing 1983
Reprinted 1983 (five times)

British Library Cataloguing in Publication Data
Sinclair, Ian
Commodore 64 computing
1. Commodore 64 (Computer)
I. Title
001.64′04   QA76.8.C/

ISBN 0-246-12030-4

Typeset by V & M Graphics Ltd, Aylesbury, Bucks
Printed and bound in Great Britain
by Mackays of Chatham, Kent

Contents

Preface

Any manual for a computer can carry only a limited amount of information, and the manual for the Commodore 64 is unusually brief. A computer is a more complex device than a toaster or a washing machine, and a full-scale encyclopaedia would be needed to explain in detail every possible action and application of a machine like the Commodore 64. Computer manuals are therefore a compromise, listing the computer actions in enough detail to allow the experienced user to work out the rest. In the case of the Commodore 64, it is likely that the user will have had experience of previous Commodore machines, so that the style of operating the machine will not seem so novel as it would to anyone who has not used a PET or a VIC–20. This, however, is of little comfort to the absolute beginner, or to anyone who has come to the 64 from another type of machine.

This book is intended to be used along with the Commodore 64 manual; with the manual acting as an appendix of data to be used along with the book. It is intended to offer the beginner a helping hand in learning the BASIC programming language which is built into the 64, and in understanding how the machine can be used with other programs. At the same time it will act as a guide for anyone who has come to the 64 after some experience on a different type of machine.

This is not a book of computer programs, nor is it devoted to 'blob-chasing' games. The program examples that appear are short and simple. The aim is to help you, the reader, to understand computer action, not to dazzle you with elaborate programs nor to wear out your typing finger(s) with long examples. By working through the examples in this book, however, you should end up with a sound knowledge of what the Commodore 64 can do, and how you can use it. That is my aim, and I hope it meets with your approval. In particular, I have emphasised the data processing uses of the machine, in the belief that the 64 will have considerable appeal for business users because of its memory size and the vast range of suitable programs (software), together with the range of printers and disk units which are available now. I have not, however, neglected the aspects of colour graphics and sound, which have been dealt with in detail because of the unique and rather complex method that is used to program these effects.

A book like this owes much to a lot of people who worked hard to organise it. In particular, I would like to thank Richard Miles of Granada Publishing Ltd who tirelessly pursued the objective of getting hold of a Commodore 64 at a time when machines were very scarce. I must pour out thanks also to Peter Walker, Susan Morris and Debbie Stephens, of Peter Walker Associates who made enormous efforts to ensure that I received a 64 for Christmas. I am greatly indebted to Henry Budgett, editor of *Computing Today*, for permission to use the C.T. standard symbols for graphics and other non-printable characters in this book. I also have a particular debt to acknowledge to Rod Wellburn of Commodore who volunteered to print the listings from my cassette, since I could not interface any of my printers to the 64. This has ensured that the listings are reproduced correctly, as they appear on the screen.

Ian Sinclair

Chapter One
Preliminaries

The Commodore 64 is a complete computer which needs only a TV receiver to be useful for programming. For any really serious work, however, you need to be able to record and replay programs (computer instructions), because a program ceases to exist when the computer is switched off. The two normal methods of recording (called saving) and replaying (called loading) are the use of cassettes and disks. The use of cassettes is cheaper, but the actions of loading and saving require a much longer time as compared to the same actions using disks for storage. The 64, like all Commodore models, requires a special cassette recorder which has been designed to operate only with Commodore machines. This has the considerable advantage that the setting-up difficulties users of other machines encounter when using ordinary cassette recorders do not trouble Commodore users. You cannot use an ordinary cassette recorder unless it has been considerably modified and provided with a suitable connecting cable. A few firms claim to provide suitable adaptors, but I was unable to check how well such an adaptor would work because the supplier was unable to furnish me with a sample. It makes sense, then, to use the correct Commodore type of recorder.

For serious computing purposes, particularly for business use, a floppy disk system is much more satisfactory. A floppy disk is a thin plastic disk which is coated with magnetic material (like cassette tape), and enclosed in a cardboard sheath. The cardboard protects the surface of the disk from fingerprints and other contamination, and the disk cannot easily be removed from the cardboard. When the floppy disk is inserted into the 'player', or disk drive, it is spun up to a speed of 300 revolutions per minute. A pick-up head can be placed over any part of the usable surface of the disk – there is a slot in the cardboard sheath to permit this. Signals can then be recorded or replayed at very high speed. Because any part of the exposed disk can be used, there is no rewinding problem as exists when cassettes are used, and access to any part of the disk is very rapid, a small fraction of a second. The disk system is completely controlled by the computer, and there are no adjustments to make.

Throughout this book, I'll assume that you are using a cassette recorder at present, but will probably change to a disk system later as your needs develop. The differences between the two affect only a few commands, but the cassette recorder needs more attention from you when it is used.

Connecting up

The connections that have to be made for a working system are to the power supply, the TV and the storage system, which I'll assume

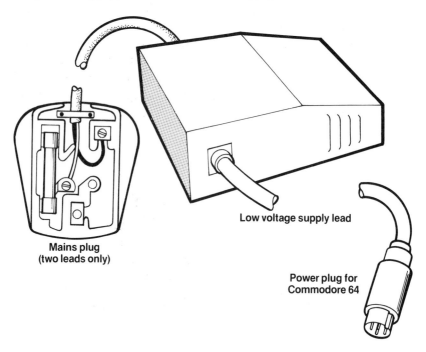

Low voltage supply lead

Mains plug
(two leads only)

Power plug for
Commodore 64

Fig. 1.1. The power connections. The high-voltage connection is to a mains plug – use a 3-amp fuse. The low voltage is to a special 4-pin plug.

will be the cassette recorder. The power supply for the UK version of the 64 is a grey metal box (a transformer) which has a mains lead on one side and a low-voltage lead for the 64 on the other side. In the United States the transformer is housed in a black plastic box. This low voltage lead is fitted with a special plug (Fig. 1.1) which pushes into a socket on the right-hand side panel of the 64. It is a good idea to keep this plug in place once the system is fitted up, because frequent insertion and removal will eventually loosen the contacts and may eventually cause intermittent loss of power. Though this will not harm the computer, it will cause loss of any program that you happen to be working on at the time. There is a power switch on the 64, close to the power socket, but this switches only the low voltage supply, not the mains. At the end of a computing session you should always switch off the mains socket or remove the mains plug. If you do not do this, the separate transformer unit of the 64 will still be operating whether the machine is switched on or not. Though the transformer is constructed so as to withstand this continuous operation, and should not overheat, I always prefer to switch off all mains supplies when they are not in use. Incidentally, the transformer must be placed where there will be a free flow of air around it, so that it will not overheat.

The other sockets on the same side of the 64 casing are for use with games accessories, such as joysticks and controllers, and also for light-pens, which allow the user to carry out actions like choosing an item simply by pointing the pen to the appropriate part of the TV screen. The light-pen can also be very useful in generating graphics displays.

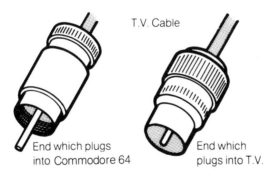

Fig. 1.2. The TV connection cable. A different cable is needed for a video monitor.

The picture signal connectors (Fig. 1.2) are at the back of the 64. There are two sets, depending on whether you wish to use an ordinary TV receiver or a 'video monitor', also called a VDU (Visual Display Unit). A monitor is a high-quality variety of TV display which does not need to use the coded signals that are normally transmitted – it cannot therefore be used as a TV receiver operating from an aerial. It will, however, accept signals from computers or video recorders, and produce pictures which are very much clearer and better focused than can ever be obtained from ordinary TV receivers. All computers that are intended for, or can be used for, serious business purposes feature a signal output for a monitor, because a computer that is likely to be used for eight or more hours per day needs a display that is less visually tiring than that of a TV receiver. The output for these signals is a 5-pin socket on the back panel, next to the TV aerial cable connector. Suitable plugs for these and the other sockets can be obtained from any of the large number of Commodore dealers.

If a video monitor is used, there is no setting-up to do apart from ensuring that its signal plug is pushed into the correct socket of the 64. A TV receiver, however, needs considerably more setting up, and if we assume that you don't have a video monitor at present, then setting up the TV receiver is the first priority.

Start by plugging the TV cable that is provided with the 64 into the correct sockets. One end plugs into the aerial socket of your TV receiver and the other end into the 64. Switch the TV receiver on, and also switch on the 64. Unless you are lucky, you won't see any picture, because the 64 contains a miniature TV transmitter, called a modulator, which is transmitting on one particular TV channel. On US versions of the 64, this channel can be changed by a switch situated next to the TV output socket of the 64, in case of possible interference. There is no external provision for changing channels on the European versions of the 64, however, and you will have to retune the TV to find this signal.

This is simple enough if you have done it before or if you are using a black/white (B/W) receiver which has variable tuning. Variable tuning in this sense means that different transmitting stations are selected by turning a dial on the front or the side of the TV, so that all you have to do is to turn this dial (see Fig. 1.4a) until the 64 tuning signal appears bright and clear. Most tuner dials of this type have a 'fine-tune' section which can be turned to make very small adjustments to the tuning. Adjust the dial until the signal has no trace of 'ghosting' and is steady and clear (Fig. 1.3).

Most colour receivers , and a number of B/W receivers, use push-button tuners. Select a button that is not used for TV reception in your district, and push it right in. This selects a channel, but it probably isn't one that will receive the 64 signal. To adjust the tuning, you will have to find out what method is used on your TV.

COMMODORE

Light coloured blobs between letters

'Ghost' images
after a letter

Fuzzy letter shape

Fig. 1.3. Picture flaws caused by faulty tuning.

Some older receivers require the tuning push-buttons to be rotated (Fig. 1.4b), more modern receivers have a panel of tuning controls (Fig. 1.4c) and you will have to find which of these controls corresponds to the button that you have pressed. Once you find it, adjust the tuning until the picture appears to be clear and steady. The adjustment of the tuning control is very critical, and very small changes will have a large effect on the picture.

If you have used a colour receiver, the picture will appear as light blue letters, with a light blue border and a dark blue background. A colour TV needs much more careful tuning than a B/W receiver, and will never display pictures as clear and well-focused as a good B/W receiver. Even for business purposes, however, the use of a colour receiver can at times be justified to produce graphical displays like bar charts. The dual signal outlets of the 64 permit the use of a colour receiver for such displays along with the use of a high-quality B/W monitor for programming use, so that it is possible to have the best of both worlds. In addition, of course, the TV output is valuable for educational, display and conference use since it can supply signals to a large screen TV or to a video recorder for later display.

An interesting feature of the 64 is that it can transmit signals to the sound section of a TV receiver in addition to the picture circuits. This facility is primarily intended for games programs, but it can be a useful 'attention-getter' for the programmer or in the course of computer generated demonstrations or other displays.

Having set up the computer and the TV receiver, we have a working system but to complete the system we need a cassette recorder or a disk system. These both make use of the connections at the back of the 64, and the computer must always be switched off when these connections are made. The cassette recorder is connected to the flat 6-pin socket which is next to the 'user port'; the disk

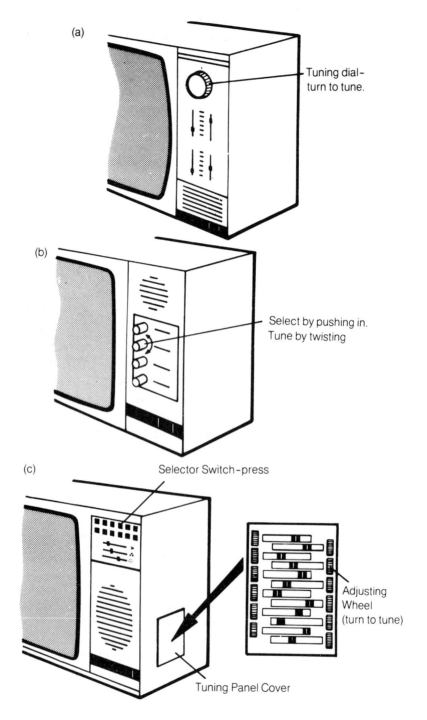

(a) Tuning dial –
turn to tune.

(b) Select by pushing in.
Tune by twisting

(c) Selector Switch – press

Adjusting
Wheel
(turn to tune)

Tuning Panel Cover

Fig. 1.4. Common types of TV tuning circuits.

system connects to the other 6-pin connector (the serial port), which is also used for the Commodore printer. For the moment, we'll defer the subject of checking out the cassette or disk system, because we need to try out the keyboard first.

The keyboard

Viewed from above, the keyboard of the 64 is laid out in a pattern that closely resembles that of a typewriter. The top row of keys, looking for the moment at the markings on the tops of the keys, carries the number digits, along with some symbols, and also has the keys marked CLR/HOME and INST/DEL at the right hand side. The next row contains the Q to P keys, exactly following the type-writer pattern, with @* ↑ and two important computer-control keys, marked CTRL (control) at the left and RESTORE at the right. The next line of keys contains keys A to L, with brackets, colon, semi-colon and equality sign. This row also has the RUN/STOP and the SHIFT LOCK keys on the left, and the RETURN key on the right. The RETURN key is a way of signalling to the computer that you have completed an instruction or action, so this key position is one that you will have to find frequently. The final row of keys contains Z to M, with the < and > marks, period (full stop), and comma, question mark and divide sign (/) and the SHIFT keys. On the left of this row is the Commodore key, marked with the ⊂ logo, which is a selection key. On the right hand side is the pair of 'cursor' shift keys which are used in editing. The final key, under this line, is the large space-bar key which once again, is identical in style and use to the typewriter space-bar.

In general, then, the special keys which are peculiar to computing are located to the left or right of the normal typewriter keys, and we can use the other keys, the letter and digit keys, just as we would use the keys of a typewriter. It's important to realise at this stage that random pressing of keys cannot damage your computer, though it may cause a stored program to be wiped out. The only way that you can physically damage the computer is by maltreatment, such as spilling coffee over it, or by making incorrect connections to the sockets. When you connect attachments you should always have the computer switched off, and you should be particularly careful of attaching any non-Commodore devices.

The characters

No, this isn't the cast-list for a play, it's a description of the shapes that appear on the screen when you press keys. When you switch on the 64 pressing any of the letter keys will produce the 'upper-case' or capital letter version of that key on the screen. The position of the letter on the screen before you type it is indicated by the 'cursor', a flashing white block. When you type a letter, the letter replaces the cursor, and the cursor moves one space to the right, indicating the position of the next letter. At the end of a line, you do *not* have to press a 'carriage return' key – the cursor will automatically move to the left hand side of the next line down. This point is important, because the RETURN key of the computer has a very different action as compared to the carriage return of a typewriter.

The reason for the automatic selection of upper-case letters is that we normally write programs in upper-case letters, and the 64 therefore sets up this condition when it is switched on. If you press either of the two SHIFT keys at the same time as you press a letter key, you will *not* get a lower-case (small) letter, but a graphics character. The graphics character that will appear on the screen will be the one that is printed on the front right-hand side of the key. For example, SHIFT and Q, which we can write as ∧Q, gives the symbol ● .

The Commodore key (marked with the ⊂ logo) allows these key actions to be changed. If you press the ⊂ key and the SHIFT key together, the 64 keyboard will from then on behave like an ordinary typewriter keyboard, on which the keys give the lower-case letters when the SHIFT is not pressed, and give upper-case letters when the SHIFT key *is* pressed. This mode of use is handy when you have to type instructions into programs, or for messages, and is indispensable when using word-processing. In this mode, if the ⊂ key is pressed along with a letter key, then the graphic symbol that is illustrated on the left hand side of the front of the key will appear on the screen. The keyboard can be restored to normal program mode by pressing the ⊂ key and SHIFT together once more. The ⊂ key can also be used along with the CTRL key to produce colour displays, a topic that we shall deal with more fully in Chapter Seven.

Keyboard use

For the first few chapters of this book, we shall concentrate on the use of the keyboard for learning to program, leaving special effects like graphics, colour and sound until later. We shall also leave the action of the special 'user-programmable' keys, the four keys at the right hand side of the keyboard, until Chapter Eight.

In programming mode, as we have just seen, the letter keys give upper-case (capital) letters, and the keys which show one symbol above another, such as you see on the top row of keys, will give the lower symbol unless the SHIFT key is also pressed. If you are familiar with the use of a typewriter, you will be familiar with this idea, but it needs to be said in case you have never used a typewriter. The same applies to the three action keys that are labelled RUN/STOP, CLR/HOME and INST/DEL – I have used the oblique stroke here in place of writing one word over the other. The same system is also found on the keys that are marked CRSR (cursor control keys).

Of these keys, the CLR/HOME is a cursor and screen control key. When the key is pressed by itself, the action is 'HOME' meaning that the cursor is returned to the top left hand corner of the screen. If the SHIFT key is used at the same time as the CLR/HOME key, then the action is to clear the screen as well as placing the cursor in the HOME position. This is a useful way of getting rid of any clutter on the screen, and preparing for a programming session.

The INST/DEL key is a vital editing key, which allows anything that you have typed to be altered. DEL means delete, and its action is to wipe out the character on the immediate left hand side of the cursor. It's a back-space-and-erase key of the type which on some other computers is marked with a left-arrow. You must not expect the left-arrow cursor key of the 64 to carry out this action. If you delete a character which is followed by other characters, then the action of deletion will also move all the characters to the right of the cursor so that they fill in the gap as Fig. 1.5 shows. When the INST/DEL key is pressed at the same time as the SHIFT key, the action is INSerT. A space is inserted at the cursor position, shifting all the following characters to the right, as shown in Fig. 1.6. A space is inserted at the cursor position so that if a letter has been omitted in a word, it can now be put into its correct place.

When you are typing and you notice an error, the delete action is usually the easiest method of correcting the mistake. When the error is near to the start of a line of characters, and deleting would mean removing a lot of typed material, the cursor movement keys can be used to place the cursor, with no effect on the characters, where the error can be dealt with. The CRSR keys, used by themselves, will move the cursor to the right or downwards. Used along with the

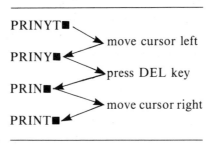

Fig. 1.5. Deleting a character. To *change* a character you need only place the cursor over it and type a new character.

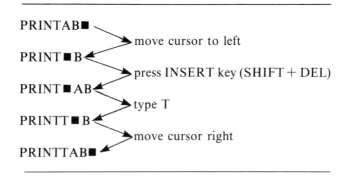

Fig. 1.6. Inserting a space between characters.

SHIFT key, the cursor keys will move the cursor left or upwards (the usual directions for correcting an error). If a CRSR key is held down, with or without the SHIFT key, then its action repeats, so that you do not have to keep stabbing at the keys to move the cursor several characters along a line or several lines up or down. When the cursor is in place, you can use DEL to delete the character *on the left of the cursor*, or you can replace the character under the cursor by typing a new character, or you can make a space by using INST, and then fill it with a new character.

The RUN/STOP key is used to a lesser extent. The action of the key, when used alone is to stop a program, and we deal with this use in Chapter Four. The RUN action should not be confused with the word 'RUN' typed (one letter at a time) as a command. The RUN key (SHIFT and RUN/STOP) is used to cause a tape to be loaded and its program run automatically.

NOTE: Always ensure that the cursor has been moved down to a vacant line before typing a new line or a command (like LIST, RUN). Failure to do this will result in an error message.

The RESTORE key is used in conjunction with the RUN/STOP key to reset the machine to the state of waiting to run a program. This is necessary in three particular cases. One is when the machine uses the instruction INPUT (see Chapter Two), and you wish to break off the program at that point. This cannot be done by using the RUN/STOP key by itself, only by using the RESTORE key as well. This is a safety precaution to prevent an inexperienced operator from stopping a program accidentally. Another use concerns the sound system. It is possible for the machine to stop with a sound signal being sent out, and the use of RESTORE with RUN/STOP will cut off this signal. Similarly, if a program leaves the screen with a colour display, possibly with the text invisible (because it is the same colour as the background), then RESTORE and RUN/STOP will cause a return to normal appearance. The two keys must be tapped sharply – it is *not* sufficient to press them gently.

Saving and loading

Until you have saved and reloaded a program, you cannot be sure that the cassette or disk system of the 64 is acting correctly. The cassette system in particular needs to be checked fairly carefully, especially if you are trying to use a non-Commodore recorder with an adaptor. Before we can test the action, however, we need a program. Press the RUN/STOP and RESTORE keys together, which will clear the screen and restore normal operation regardless of any other keys that you may have pressed previously. Now type the simple program that is illustrated in Fig. 1.7. The word REM

```
1Ø REM
2Ø REM
3Ø REM
4Ø REM
```

Fig. 1.7. A simple 'program' for testing cassette recorder action.

means reminder, and it's a signal word to the computer that what follows is not an instruction. The 'program' consists of four lines that are numbered 1∅,2∅,3∅ and 4∅, and the word REM. Don't omit the numbers – that's what makes it a program, even though it does not do anything. You will have to press the RETURN key after each line is complete (after the M of REM). After the last line has been typed and RETURN pressed, type the words:

SAVE"TEST"

and then press the RETURN key. The computer will then print on the screen:

PRESS PLAY AND RECORD ON TAPE

and your response to this should be to press these keys on the recorder, holding the RECORD key down first, then the PLAY, and pressing them hard enough to be sure that they lock in place. The screen will clear while the computer is recording your program on to the tape, and the word READY will appear when recording is complete. You can then press the STOP key of the recorder. If you are using a non-Commodore recorder with an adaptor, you will have to follow the instructions that come with the adaptor unit to see what sequence will be needed.

You can now test the efficacy of recording. Switch off the computer, and then switch on again. When you have switched on again, type LIST and then press the RETURN key. Nothing new should appear, indicating that there is no program in the computer. Now rewind the tape, and type:

LOAD"TEST"

and then press RETURN. The screen will then show the message:

PRESS PLAY ON TAPE

As before, if you are using the Commodore recorder, pressing its PLAY key so that it locks in place will start the tape running, and the screen of the computer will clear. The computer is now looking for the recording of the name of the program, TEST. When this is found, the message:

FOUND TEST

will appear, and you can load the program by pressing the ⊂ key. If you decided that you didn't want to load this program, you could press the RUN/STOP key instead. Once the program has loaded, the

READY

prompt signal will reappear, and typing LIST followed by pressing RETURN should make your program reappear on the screen. If you don't press any keys when the FOUND message appears, then the program will be loaded after a short delay.

Once again, if you are using a cassette recorder which is not a Commodore type, along with an adaptor, you will have to follow the instructions that come with the adaptor. In addition, you will have to set the volume control of the cassette recorder, using cut-and-try methods. In general, a volume control setting of about halfway, with any tone control set at a maximum treble, will be a good starting point, but you may have to attempt several loads with slightly different volume control settings in order to achieve satisfactory loading. When you have found a satisfactory position, mark it! Users of the Commodore machine have no volume controls to worry about.

Disk storing and loading

The use of disks is rather beyond the scope of this book, but brief advice on the saving and loading of programs may be useful. In general, saving and loading on disk are both operations that are simpler than corresponding cassette operations. You must first ensure that a disk has been placed in the disk drive, correct way up. Starting once again with the four-line program of Fig. 1.7 type:

SAVE"TEST",8

and then press RETURN. The digit 8 is the reference number for the disk system – this is the only way in which the computer can distinguish a cassette SAVE operation from a disk SAVE operation. The disk drive will start to spin the disk, and you will see appearing in quick succession on the screen the messages:

SAVING"TEST"
OK
READY

When the READY signal has appeared, the program is saved and you can turn off the computer (check your disk drive manual about the procedure for turning off the computer when the disk drive is fitted). Turn on the system again, and type LIST (followed by pressing RETURN) to ensure that no program is present, then type:

LOAD"TEST",8

Press RETURN, and the disk drive will start, then the messages:

SEARCHING FOR TEST
LOADING
READY

will appear. You can then LIST (press RETURN) to see the four-line program displayed. Note that a new disk has to be 'formatted', and a formatted disk has to be 'initialised' before being used. For the meaning of these words, and the methods of achieving these actions, see the disk-user manual.

Using cartridges

A range of programs, and particularly programs for business purposes as well as for games, will be available on cartridge. The cartridge contains additional memory of a permanent kind, and by plugging in this cartridge, you are connecting this pre-programmed memory into the main memory of the computer. To use the cartridge, first switch off the computer and all of its attachments. Insert the cartridge into the large slot at the back of the computer – the one with eleven contacts. Now switch the computer on. Read the instruction sheet that comes with the cartridge – this will tell you which key on the 64 you will have to press to start the cartridge program running. Normally, either the C= key or the RUN key (SHIFT with RUN/STOP) will be used for this purpose.

Chapter Two
Beginning BASIC

If your computer-owning days started with a Commodore machine such as the PET or the more recent VIC–20, then this chapter and the three following will have few surprises for you, because Commodore have very sensibly retained the same BASIC for the 64 as they used in the earlier models. BASIC is the computing language that was developed for easy learning, and though some manufacturers pride themselves on using an 'extended BASIC' that is much more difficult to learn and to use, Commodore have retained the original simplicity of BASIC. The reason is that the 64 can make use of a variety of languages, so that anyone who needs to use a different language in order to do different things has only to plug in a different language chip or cartridge.

The 64 may, however, be your wise first choice of computer by consideration of price, availability, the huge range of add-on extras and the equally large range of software that is available *now* (not at some promised time in the future!), ease of use, potential for development, and all the other points that make this such an excellent machine. If this is so, you probably don't know any BASIC, and this chapter, with the three that follow, will help you. Learning BASIC is like learning any other language. There are rules, called *syntax*, and there are words, the *keywords*, which have to be learned and used. The difference between BASIC and a 'foreign' language is that BASIC has very few words for you to learn, and the rules are simple, with no confusing exceptions. The easiest way to learn BASIC, like any other language, is by using it. You should therefore try out everything that is suggested in this and the following chapters on your own machine. In this way you become familiar with the keyboard and with the commands of the machine very much faster than you would simply by reading.

Direct commands

To start with, a command can be issued by typing a command word, or keyword, followed by pressing the RETURN key. Nothing happens when you type words – the action is always started by the use of the RETURN key, because this is the 'get-it-done' key. Until you press RETURN, you can change what you have typed as much as you like, but pressing RETURN carries out the action very rapidly – if it can be done. Try it – type:

PRINT 2.6 − 1.1   (now press RETURN)

The result 1.5 printed on the screen below the characters PRINT 2.6 − 1.1. The keyword in this example is PRINT, meaning print-a-new-line-of-information-on-the-screen. If we want to print on paper, we need to specify this in a different way, and we shall look at this in Chapter Five.

The computer does as you instruct it; it can't read your thoughts. If you type simply: 2.6 − 1.1 = (with no PRINT instruction), then when you press RETURN, you will find that the computer ignores what you have typed. You will have disobeyed a rule of computer grammar, which is that the first part of a command must be an instruction word taken from the list of BASIC instruction words given in the manual. The number 2.6 isn't an instruction word, and the computer can make no sense of it. You're dealing with a machine, not a thinking, guessing, human. Type NEW and press RETURN to remove the error.

Symbol	Use	Example
+	positive number	+6
−	negative number	−5
↑	raise to power	$3 ↑ 2 = 9$ ($3^2 = 9$)
*	multiply by	$5 * 6 = 30$
/	divide by	$81/3 = 27$
+	add to	$5 + 4 = 9$
−	subtract from	$17 − 8 = 9$

These are listed in order of precedence.

Fig. 2.1. The arithmetic symbols that are used for the 64.

The way that we used PRINT was as a direct command, and you could use the 64 just as a calculator, with the arithmetic symbols that are illustrated in the table of Fig. 2.1. You didn't buy a 64 just to use it as a calculator, though, so we'll leave the subject of direct commands for the moment and move to programming. The difference is that a direct command is carried out whenever the RETURN key is pressed. If you want to repeat the same command, you have to type it all again and press RETURN again, which is tedious. The computer provides a better method, program mode.

A program *instruction* is distinguished from a direct command because it starts with a number rather than with a command word. The number must be a positive whole number like 1,10,98, (not -12 or $+13.7$), and the range of numbers that you can use is from 0 to 63999. Your computer will use these numbers in two ways:

(1) To indicate that what follows is a set of instructions that are to be carried out later,
(2) to show in what order the instructions are to be carried out.

If you have three instructions in three lines that are numbered 1, 2, and 3, then the instructions will be carried out in ascending order of these line numbers from 1 to 3. As it happens, using 1, 2, 3 numbering is inconvenient because if we need an extra instruction between lines we can't fit it into place so easily (we can't use line 1.5) so we generally use numbers that rise in tens, such as 1∅,2∅,3∅, ... and so on.

When we start with a number then, the computer does not carry out the instruction when we press RETURN, it simply *stores* the instruction(s) in its memory and waits for more. You still need to press RETURN when you have finished typing a complete instruction line, but RETURN causes storage, not execution of the instructions. To execute the instructions, you need to use a new *command* word, RUN.

Note, incidentally, that a 'line' in this sense does not mean one line on the screen. It means whatever you type following a line number right up until the point when you press RETURN. This can make several lines of text on the screen, and you must *not* be tempted to press RETURN when you see the letters reaching the right hand side of the screen. The computer will automatically place letters on a new screen line as you continue to type; if you press RETURN, this will be taken as the end of the instruction. This is slightly difficult to grasp if you are an experienced typist!

Now try the example in Fig. 2.2. It's a three-line program, so that

```
10 PRINT 2.3+1.6
20 PRINT 4.7*2.25
30 PRINT 16.3/2.4
```

Fig. 2.2. A simple arithmetic program.

when you have finished entering line 3Ø all that you will see on the screen will be the program lines that you typed, not the answers. If you want to see the program lines repeated, type the *command* word LIST (then press RETURN). The program will run (be carried out) if you type the word RUN and then press RETURN. Once again, notice how RETURN is used to cause the command to be carried out.

Now try this one – type a new line which has the number 15. You can make it something like:

15 PRINT 6.7 − 2.6   (press RETURN)

On the screen *at the moment* the line appears under the others, but it has been stored in such a way that it will be carried out between lines 1Ø and 2Ø, where its line number places it. To see how the computer has arranged these lines in its memory, type again the word LIST and press RETURN. You will now see the lines arranged in their correct order.

More print actions

So far, we've printed only the answers to arithmetic problems. The PRINT instruction is capable of much more than this, however, and it's the main way in which we get information from the computer. To extend its use, we add other marks, called print modifiers, to the PRINT instruction. To start with, we can use inverted commas, or quotes (""). When you follow a PRINT instruction with quotes, then anything placed between the quotes is printed *exactly as it appears between the quotes*. Try the example in Fig. 2.3. When you RUN this one, the first action is to print the word ARITHMETIC. Under

```
10 PRINT"ARITHMETIC"
20 PRINT
30 PRINT"2 TIMES 6 IS ";2*6
```

Fig. 2.3. Printing words as well as results.

this is a space, a blank line, because nothing followed the word PRINT in line 2∅. When you use PRINT, the computer always selects a new screen line to print on, unless you instruct it otherwise. The third line reads 2 TIMES 6 IS 12 when the program runs (did you put a space between the S of IS and the second quote mark?). You haven't put the number 12 into your program, it was calculated. The items outside the quotes are calculations, the items inside the quotes are printed as they are, literally. Such items that are placed between quotes are called string literals – any set of characters that you like to type. These string literals put between quotes will always be printed exactly as you typed them.

So far, each time we use PRINT, the computer takes a new line to print on. We can suppress that action by adding a semicolon (;) sign after a printed item, outside the last quote mark. For example, if we type the short program in Fig. 2.4, then when we RUN this we shall

```
10 PRINT"USING";
20 PRINT" THE";
30 PRINT" SEMICOLON"
```

Fig. 2.4. How semicolons alter the effect of PRINT.

see the message printed on one line – the semicolon has prevented the new line from being taken. The use of the semicolon will also suppress spaces, so that if you type:

    1∅ PRINT "THIS"   "ONE"

(using the space-bar to create the spaces), and RUN this, you will see THISONE – the space that was between the words does not appear in the printed output. If you want to make spaces appear, they must be placed *inside* the quotes.

Did you find that this program produced more than you expected? If you have had a program stored in memory from a previous exercise, then some lines from that program will still be present. This can be a nuisance, so to remove such unwanted programs before you start typing in a new one, you can type NEW (then press RETURN) so as to clear the way for your new items.

The comma (,) also serves to modify the PRINT instruction, but in a rather different way. Try the program in Fig. 2.5. When you RUN this, the four letters are spread over the line, spaced out equally. The comma causes a space of ten letter widths to be allocated to each item between the commas, so that the width of the screen, which will accommodate 40 letters or digits (or other

```
10 PRINT"A","B","C","D"
```

Fig. 2.5. The effect of using commas.

characters) is split into four columns. If you take up too much space for one item, then the next column can't be used for another item – try the example in Fig. 2.6. The first item here is too long to fit into a ten-

```
10 PRINT"MUCH TOO LONG","B","C","D"
```

Fig. 2.6. If one item is too long, the fields are rearranged.

letter wide column, so the next column cannot start at the eleventh space, and must start at the twenty-first space. This leaves only two columns for "B" and "C", so that "D" has to be printed on the next line. This use of commas provides a simple way of making neat columns of items that need fewer than ten spaces, however. Try the lines in Fig. 2.7 which will arrange the words so that they fall into

```
10 PRINT"THIS IS","SO IS","ANOTHER","THE FINAL"
20 PRINT"A TITLE","THIS ONE","TITLE","TITLE"
```

Fig. 2.7. Printing in four columns.

four columns, but arranged as two lines. See how the computer has printed the first four items across the screen, then printed the next four directly underneath. This is a particularly useful way of arranging columns for display purposes; it's a most useful feature for classification, for example.

By this time, incidentally, you will have noticed that when you type a new line 1∅, the previous line of that number is replaced. Even if you simply type 1∅ and then press RETURN, you will have removed any line 1∅ that previously existed. Wiping a line is just one way of altering what you have typed, and the use of NEW will remove a whole program. From now on, we shall use another instruction which clears the screen of the clutter of old program lines that accumulated there. You will now have seen that the screen 'scrolls' – the printed items on the screen move upward to make room for new items, and eventually disappear from the top of the screen. This is one way of removing unwanted lines, but the PRINT "CLR" instruction (CLear Screen) will provide you with a blank screen at any stage in a program. We have already seen the use of the CLR key on the keyboard to do the same thing. Neither the CLR key nor the PRINT "CLR" instruction remove anything from the memory of the computer – your program is still safely stored. Note that "CLR" appears on the screen as an inverse heart symbol.

We've seen that the spacing of columns on the screen can be organised by using the commas outside quote marks. There's another way of organising spacing which is more controllable – the instruction TAB. TAB means tabulate, meaning move across the screen to some position. You have to specify what that position is by typing a number following TAB, and the numbering is done in the same way as on a typewriter, by starting from the left hand side of the screen. Computers usually start number counts with $\emptyset$ rather than 1, so the tabulation numbers start at $\emptyset$ and end at 39, since the 64 uses a screen 'width' of 40 characters – this is referred to as a '40 column screen'. The number that follows TAB must be enclosed within brackets (parenthesis) – try the example in Fig. 2.8. By using

```
10 PRINTTAB(17)"TITLE"
20 PRINT:PRINT
30 PRINTTAB(1)"THIS SHOWS HOW A TITLE CAN BE
PLACED"
40 PRINTTAB(5)"IN THE CENTRE OF THE SCREEN."
```

Fig. 2.8. Using TAB to position the start of printing.

TAB(17) for the first item, the word TITLE is placed in the centre of the screen. There's no magic about finding the number, just a calculation that typists have been using for generations – it's illustrated in Fig. 2.9.

---

1. Count the number of letters and spaces in the title   Example: 14
2. Divide this by 2, and round up if there is a remainder   Example: 7
3. Subtract this number from 19   Example: 13
4. Use this as the TAB number.

Fig. 2.9. How to calculate the value for TAB.

Another point to note about this particular program is that it has two instructions in line $2\emptyset$, separated by a colon (:). This is called a 'multi-statement line', and it achieves the same effect as having two lines with the instruction PRINT in each. The instructions in a multi-statement line like this are executed in the order that you read the line, from left to right, and there is a limit – you can't have more than 80 characters (letters, digits, spaces, punctuation marks) in a line. You must also place the colon after each 'statement', where you would normally have taken a new line and pressed RETURN. The advantage of using lines like this is that it keeps instructions grouped as you want them, and that it saves on memory space. This is because each time you take a new line, the computer has to store the address (an index to that line) in its memory, and this index entry takes up memory space.

```
10 PRINTTAB(5)"ITEM";TAB(20)"ANOTHER";TAB(35)
"ITEM"
20 PRINTSPC(5)"ITEM";SPC(20)"ANOTHER";SPC(10)
"ITEM"
```

Fig. 2.10. TAB and SPC contrasted.

There are two more ways in which we can modify PRINT, but we use them rather less than TAB. One is SPC, which will print a number of spaces. How many? As many as we specify within brackets following SPC – the limit is 255. This is useful if we want a fixed number of spaces following an item, as illustrated in Fig. 2.10 which contrasts the effects of TAB and SPC. Another instruction word that is concerned with the PRINT position on a line is POS. This finds the position along the line where the next item will be printed – but we'll leave that one for the moment.

Variables

By this time you are probably wondering if you ought to have taken a course in typing before you learned BASIC, since every serious computer requires the use of some typing skills. Fortunately, it's possible to reduce the amount of typing, and gain some other advantages, by using what we call 'variables'. A variable is a code of one or two letters, and like any other code, we can decide what our variable will represent. Take a look at Fig. 2.11. In line 1∅, which is another multi-statement line, we have allocated (or *assigned*) two variable names. This simply means that we have decided what letter codes we shall use for two items. One item is the name SMITH, and it has been allocated the code SN$. The SN part is the unique code, the dollar sign, called a string in computing lingo, is a signal to the computer that we are using the letters SN here to mean a 'string', a set of letters rather than a number. The reason for specifying this is

```
10 SN$="SMITH":T$="THIS NAME IS"
20 PRINT T$;" DONALD";" ";SN$
30 PRINT T$;" KIRSTIE";" ";SN$
40 PRINT T$;" GORDON";" ";SN$
50 PRINT T$;" SARAH";" ";SN$
```

Fig. 2.11. Using variables to represent words.

that the same code letters with no dollar sign attached would be treated as a code for a number, and the computer treats numbers very differently from the way it treats strings. You can multiply 27 by 32, for example, but you can't multiply 27 Blackberry Way by 1010 42nd St., or JONES by SMITH. Anything that you would PRINT placed between quotes will need a variable name that is followed by its dollar sign – we call this name a 'string variable'.

See how the use of string variables in Fig. 2.11 saves typing. The string variables are assigned with values in line 1∅, and the other lines make use of them. Wherever any name or set of letters is used more than once, it makes good sense to assign it to a string variable in this way. We can change this assignment any time we like – that's why it's called a variable – but the letters remain assigned until we *do* change the assignment. A very few computers require you to type the word LET when you assign a variable name with a value (such as LET A = 6, LET A$ = "NAME"). The 64 follows the world-wide MICROSOFT standard which does not require this word to be used. If you type LET, however, the computer will not reject it.

```
10 SN$="SINCLAIR":SN=1.667:SN%=2446
20 PRINT"SN$ IS ";SN$
30 PRINT"SN IS ";SN
40 PRINT"SN% IS ";SN%
```

Fig. 2.12. Three different types of variables can use the same letters (name).

In addition to string variables, we can assign two types of number variables. We can even use the *same code letters* for the two different types of number variable and the string variable, providing that we remember to use the distinguishing marks! Just to take an example in Fig. 2.12, SN$ is a string variable, SN is an ordinary number (called a 'real' number) and SN% is an integer number. Why the difference? An integer is a positive whole number whose value lies between -32768 and $+32767$ and the usefulness of it is that the computer can store numbers of this type very compactly, taking up only two units (called bytes) of its memory. It can also carry out work on these numbers very quickly, much more quickly than it can deal with numbers like −27.64, 136.43 or 1.2E-7, which are the 'real' numbers. Real numbers need a lot more memory for storage, five units each in fact.

One point in particular that you need to be aware of is that arithmetic using integers is always exact, but when real numbers are used, the answers are practically *never* exact! The error may be only in the tenth decimal place, and not visible on the screen, but it does mean that you have to take some care with involved calculations. We'll look at this point in more detail in Chapter Three. Note, by the way, at this point, that some variable names are 'illegal' – they are reserved for use by the 64. Normally we can use any combination of letters, or letter and digit provided that the first character is a letter. Fig. 2.13 is a list of variable names that are used in a special way by the 64, and which we should not use for other purposes. If you try to use these variable names, you will find that their values change as the program progresses!

ST Used when data is replayed from a cassette
TI Used as a timer
TI$ Used to hold six 'time of day' characters.

In addition, several two letter names which are reserved words (like GO, TO) or which are the first two letters of reserved words, cannot be used.

Fig. 2.13. Reserved variable names – the use of these will be rejected.

Inputs to programs

So far, on the program examples that we have looked at, we have programmed so as to produce outputs which take the form of printing on the screen. We can also provide for *inputs*, which allow the computer to suspend a program until you have typed some number, word, or phrase. This 'input' might for example, be an answer to a question that has been printed on the screen, and we signal that our reply is complete by pressing the RETURN key. The instruction word that produces this effect is INPUT, and its use is illustrated in Fig. 2.14. Whatever you type as a reply to the question of line 1∅ has to be allocated to a variable name – you can't have a line which simply consists of the word INPUT. Since what you are going to replay is a name rather than a number, the variable name that we use must be a name with the string sign attached; a string

```
10 PRINT"WHAT IS YOUR NAME"
20 INPUT NM$
30 PRINT NM$;" ,I LIKE IT"
```

Fig. 2.14. Using INPUT to type a reply to a question.

variable name. Line 3∅ then simply demonstrates that this variable name has been allocated.

There are several unexpected points about the use of INPUT. One is that when the computer comes to line 2∅, it will take a new line on the screen, place a question mark (query) at the start of that line, and wait. It will wait for as long as it has to, because unless you signal by pressing RETURN that you have completed your input, it will stay in this waiting state. When the variable that is being used is a string variable, then *any* item that you type, number or letter, as long as it does not contain more than 255 characters, will be accepted.

If you type nothing, and simply press RETURN, the computer takes this as meaning a blank, and the PRINT NM$ instruction (with nothing else but NM$ printed) will then print a blank line on the screen. In line 3∅ of the example, only the words ', I LIKE IT' will appear.

Another point about the INPUT instruction is that you don't need to place quotes around the name that you type in response to the query. It is only when you allocate a string variable name to a string within a program line that you need the quotes. If you add quotes to the item that you type, then these quotes will be taken as part of the item, and will appear when it is printed.

```
10 PRINT"YOUR NAME, PLEASE";
20 INPUT NM$
30 PRINT"I KNEW A ";NM$;" ONCE."
```

Fig. 2.15. A neater form of INPUT, using the same line.

Since the INPUT instruction is so often used as the reply to a question printed on the screen, it is natural to have PRINT and INPUT used together, with PRINT used to 'ask' the question, and INPUT to answer it. By using a semicolon, we can place both question and answer on the same line, as is illustrated in Fig. 2.15. This looks neater than having the question and the answer on

```
10 INPUT"YOUR NAME, PLEASE";NM$
20 PRINT"AT EASE,";NM$;" ,AT EASE."
```

Fig. 2.16. Combining INPUT with a printed message. Note the semicolon, which must not be omitted.

separate lines, and is so useful that the actions can be combined as illustrated in Fig. 2.16. The question is placed between quotes following the INPUT instruction word, then a semicolon is used to separate this from the variable name that we are going to allocate to the answer.

If a string variable is used, then any reply is acceptable, but if a number variable is used, then *only a number is acceptable.* In addition, the number variable must be of the correct type – it is useless to have INPUT N% and then to type 1.746 as a reply, because 1.746 is not an integer. If there is any doubt as to what the answer might be, always use a string variable. Using a number variable and then typing a string will cause the error message REDO FROM START. Unlike the action of many computers, this does not stop the program from running, it simply allows you another chance to put in the correct kind of information.

READ ... DATA

There is another way of allocating a value or a string item to a variable name, that of reading the item from a list. The list is called a data list, and it is placed into the program using the word DATA as a marker. DATA is the first word in the list following the line number. The items of the list are separated by commas (though no such separation is needed between the word DATA and the first item), and they are used only by an instruction READ placed somewhere else in the program. If the DATA line occurs early in the program, the computer simply ignores it until there is a READ instruction. This is the first exception to the rule about lines being carried out in strict sequence. If there is more than one DATA line the computer treats the higher-numbered DATA lines as simply being extensions of the first one.

```
10 DATA ALBATROSS,BAT,CUCKOO
20 READ A$:V$=" THIS ITEM IS"
30 PRINT V$;" ";A$
40 READ A$:PRINT V$;" ";A$
50 READ A$:PRINT V$;" ";A$
```

Fig. 2.17. Reading items from a DATA list.

Figure 2.17 shows this pair of instruction words being used in a program that needs rather too much typing for my taste. The DATA line is put at the start of the program, but it could have been placed at the end or in the middle, it makes no difference. The list consists of three items, and when the computer carries out line 2∅, the first of the items is used. This is printed in line 3∅, along with the phrase "THIS ITEM IS", which has been allocated to V$. Line 4∅ contains another READ instruction, and because we are reading from a list, the item that is read is the second item, which is allocated to V$ in place of ALBATROSS and so is printed in line 4∅. Similarly, line 5∅ reads the third item and prints it.

If we had a fourth READ in the program, but only three items of DATA, it would be impossible to proceed, and the computer would halt with the error message OUT OF DATA. When this happens, you *can't* resume the program from where it halted – you have to correct the fault and start again. The only error message that will still permit you to continue is the REDO FROM START message that appears when you have made an incorrect type of reply (string in place of number) to an input. If you try to READ a number variable (READ A), but have a string as data, then the computer will stop with a TYPE MISMATCH error message.

The example that has been used here is clumsy, because identical instructions have been repeated, typed and executed more than once. Note that A$ is allocated to a different word each time, so there is no reason why we should not simply repeat the same instructions three times. This type of action is called a *loop*, and we shall deal with this topic in much more detail in Chapter Four.

Sometimes we want to be able to read a list from the start again in a program which has already read the list once. This action can be ensured by using the instruction word RESTORE. This has the effect of causing any READ instruction to start once again at the first item of DATA, rather than continuing with a list, or delivering an OUT OF DATA error message. RESTORE will start the data list at the lowest numbered DATA line – some machines have the facility to RESTORE to any number line, but this is not available on the 64.

GET it?

Sometimes the use of INPUT takes too long! Typing a word and pressing RETURN is a long procedure if all you want to do is to press one key to make a choice. To make life easier for you, the 64 offers a different instruction, GET.

GET exists in the forms GET N, for a number, and GET N$ for a letter. The N and N$ are examples of variable names only, and you can use any valid variable names that you like. The effect of GET is similar to that of INPUT – the computer detects a key being pressed, but you have to arrange for the instruction to be repeated until this happens. The program then continues. You don't have to press RETURN. Of course, if you use this deliberately to enforce a wait, and print the message "PRESS ANY KEY TO PROCEED", then the RETURN key is as good as any to press. The point is that only one key needs to be pressed, not two.

```
10 PRINT"PICK A LETTER, PLEASE"
20 GET L$:IF L$=""THEN 20
30 PRINT"YES,";L$;" IS A LETTER."
40 PRINT"PICK A NUMBER, PLEASE"
50 GET L:IF L=0 THEN 50
60 PRINT"YES,";L;" IS A NUMBER."
70 PRINT"PRESS ANY KEY TO PROCEED"
80 GET L$:IF L$=""THEN 80
90 PRINT"YOU JUST DID !"
```

Fig. 2.18. Using GET in place of INPUT.

Figure 2.18 shows three common uses of GET. In line 2∅, GET L$ will accept any key that is pressed. Even though the instruction in line 1∅ is PICK A LETTER, any key will be accepted – ways of rejecting undesirable inputs are dealt with in the following chapter. In line 5∅, GET L will accept only a number, stored as a real number variable. You can also use GET L% so as to obtain an integer. GET L% is used in exactly the same way as GET L.

Lines 7∅ and 8∅ then show another use of GET. In this case, you are using GET just as a way of making the computer wait for you, not because you are interested in using the key that has been pressed or making an answer to any question. This waiting action is often useful.

Chapter Three
Processing

In Chapter Two, we saw how we can print numbers or letters on the screen and how we can put numbers or letters into the memory of the computer in the form of variable names. It's time now to look at what we can do with these inputs so as to make them into outputs – in other words, how we can process numbers and letters. We'll start with numbers. The most obvious type of processing that we probably want to carry out using numbers will be arithmetic and the solution of formulae. Processing of this type is particularly important in accounting or scientific programming, and is well provided for in the 64, making this computer an excellent choice for these activities.

We have looked previously at the arithmetic commands $+, -, *, /$ and $\uparrow$. When more than one of these instructions is used in a single instruction (called an expression), then the computer follows a definite order of precedence. For example, if you have a line:

PRINT $26 + 4.2*2.7 - 36/3.2$

then the order of carrying out the operations is *not* the same as the order of reading from left to right. The operations of multiplication and division are always performed before addition and subtraction, so that in the example above, the computer will start by calculating $4.2*2.7$ (which is 11.34) and then $36/3.2$ (which is 11.25), and then will calculate $26 + 11.34 - 11.25$ giving the answer 26.09. If the computer followed a strict left-to-right order, then $26 + 4.2 = 30.2$, then $30.2*2.7 = 81.54$, then $81.54 - 36$ gives 45.54 and $45.54/3.2 = 14.23125$, quite a different answer. If we want to ensure that the computer carries out operations in the order that we want (different from its normal order), then we have to use brackets to enforce our choice. If we wanted to use the order of writing (left to right) in the example, we would have to write it as:

$$((26 + 4.2) * 2.7 - 36)/3.2$$

What happens is that the innermost set of brackets is treated first, so that 26 + 4.2 is worked out. This result is then multiplied by 2.7 (into the outer brackets, now), and then 36 is subtracted. Finally, the result is divided by 3.2. The use of brackets will enforce any order that we choose, but otherwise the normal order of precedence is followed. Exponentiation, which is raising a number to some power like 2 (square) or 3 (cube) is given priority ahead of multiplication and division, and sign (+ or −) is accorded top priority. If all priorities are equal, then the order of carrying out operations is simply left to right.

All of these arithmetic operations can be carried out using number variables rather than with the numbers directly. This allows us to program a formula and to use INPUT so as to put in the numbers that we want to use. For example, suppose that we want to take an amount SP (selling price) and add 15% sales tax to it. We can program this as:

SP = SP + .15 * SP

which looks very curious to anyone brought up on algebra. What it means is that the new value of SP is equal to its old value plus 0.15 times its old value (15% has been expressed as 0.15). If we start with SP = 1ØØ then after this instruction has been carried out, SP will be equal to 115. This places the new value into the same variable name as we used for the old value. We don't have to do this, but it's often useful, as you will see in the course of this book.

In the course of a program which deals with calculating final prices of a number of items, you might have to carry out this operation of adding 15% on a number of different variables with different names. When this has to be done, you don't have to write a separate line for each, you can use what is called a *defined function*. A defined function is a way of writing a formula which can then be used on any variable name you care to choose. In our example, you could use the defined function that is shown in Fig. 3.1. The defined function consists of the formula, equated to the DEF FNA(SP) on the left hand side. DEF means define, FN is the abbreviation for function, A is a name, just as a variable might be named, and the SP in brackets is the variable name that is used in the formula. Whatever quantity you like can be placed between the brackets of FNA( ), and this quantity will be used in place of the SP that we put there in the definition part. When we reply to the question on sale price in line 2Ø, and type a number, this is allocated to X. By placing X in the FNA brackets in line 3Ø, as FNA(X), what we are doing is to select the formula of

```
10 DEF FNA(SP)=SP+.15*SP
20 INPUT"SALE PRICE";X
30 PRINT"FINAL PRICE IS ";FNA(X)
```

Fig. 3.1. A program which uses a defined function.

function A, as defined in line 1∅, but with X substituted for SP. We could use any other variable name we liked, the same process will be carried out on it. Only one variable name can be used within the brackets in this way. The variable can also be a 'dummy variable', meaning that it is not actually used in the formula.

```
10 DEF FNR(A)=(INT(A*100))/100
20 INPUT"NUMBER";B:PRINT FNR(B)
```

Fig. 3.2. A defined function which chops a number to two decimal places.

Figure 3.2 shows another example of a defined function in use. This example chops a figure to two decimal places, a very useful operation for financial work. This is done by multiplying by 100, removing the fraction, and then dividing by 100. Details of this operation are discussed later.

When you need to use a formula that involves more than one variable, such as calculating the long side of a right-angled triangle from the data on the other two sides, then a defined function is not quite so convenient, as its formula must contain all but one of the factors that you will use. The formula can be used directly, if it is to be used only once, or it can be programmed as a subroutine (see Chapter Four). Figure 3.3 shows this example, where the long side equals

$$\sqrt{A^2 + B^2}$$

where A and B are the lengths of the shorter sides. This program performs correctly, but you will find that the long side C has its value printed to more decimal places than could possibly be justified by the sizes of the quantities A and B. For example, if A = 3.6 and B = 4.4, then C = 5.6850681, and a value rounded to 5.7 would be more appropriate, because A and B contain only one place of decimals. If a set number of decimal places, rather than strict rounding up, is acceptable, then a defined function as shown in Fig. 3.2 can be used to round off the results. The defined function uses the instruction INT. INT means integer part, and its use will remove the fractional part from any number that follows INT within brackets. For example, if A = 3.67 then INT(A) = 3; if A = ∅.14 then INT(A)

= ∅ and so on. When A is negative, the use of INT(A) will round the number down, so that if A is −3.6, then INT(A) is −4. By using brackets in the expression of Fig. 3.2 we compel the multiplication A * 1∅∅ to be carried out first, and then the integer part taken. For example, if we take C = 5.685∅681, then carrying out this action on C, using FNR(C) will cause C * 1∅∅ = 568.5∅687 to be found, then the integer part is taken, which is 568. When this is divided by 1∅∅ again, the result is 5.68, which is the value of C taken to two decimal places with no rounding up or down. If you want the number rounded up, then the defined function that is illustrated in Fig. 3.3 is more suitable. Alternatively, by adding .∅∅5 to the figure before using the multiplication and INT, it will convert a 5.6854 to 5.69 and a 5.6844 to 5.68, so performing rounding up. To obtain more decimal places, you can use 1∅∅∅ or 1∅∅∅∅ instead of 1∅∅. If you want only one place of decimals, use 1∅ in the formula. You will have to make adjustments to the rounding portion if you use this alternative method, but if you add .5 to the number after it has been multiplied but before the use of INT, only the power of ten has to be changed in the formula.

The use of INT in this way is a useful safeguard against the small errors that are caused by the way the computer stores numbers. The numbers that are shown on the screen are always rounded up, but this is not the way in which they are stored, so that PRINT 2 * 2 will give a 4 on the screen, but the number stored may be 3.9999999999... If you have to check whether two numbers are equal, you will have to ensure that both of them are rounded to the same number of decimal places before the comparison. For example, in accounts programs, you may wish to check that the sums of two columns of figures are identical. If multiplication or division have been used, it's almost certain that they will not be *identical*, and even if only addition and subtraction have been used, it's possible that the numbers may not be absolutely identical to the last place of decimals. Since financial sums deal only with pennies, cents, mils, sous, pfennigs, you name it – there is no need to use more than two places of decimals, so that the rounding function shown in Fig. 3.3 should be used.

For scientific use, the 64 can be used to work out considerably more complex formulae than we have shown here. We shall not spend time on these, because if you understand the use of the formulae, then putting them into BASIC form for the 64 will be the least of your problems. If a formula is too complicated though, the 64 may refuse to tackle it in one step, and you will have to re-program it in steps, using one variable name allocated to the value of one part of the formula, and another variable name for another part, so that you end up with a simple function like multiplying one variable by another.

```
10 DEF FNR(A)=(INT(A*100+.5))/100
20 INPUT"SIDE 1";A
30 INPUT"SIDE 2";B
40 C=SQR(A↑2+B↑2)
50 PRINT"LONG SIDE IS ";C;" LONG"
60 PRINT"WHICH IS APPROX. ;"FNR(C)
```

Fig. 3.3. A 'triangle-solver' program which needs a defined function to round up the result to two decimal places.

String along with me

The ways in which the computer can process string variables are very different from the way in which it can process number variables. This is the reason for the distinguishing $ in the string variable name, and the quotes around strings when you type them into program lines. No arithmetic processes can be carried out on strings, but the + sign can be used to join two strings together, as Fig. 3.4 shows. This applies even if the string is a string of digits, looking like a number! If A$ = "12" and B$ = "13" then A$ + B$ = "1213", not 25. Once again, the computer treats and stores strings quite differently from the way it treats and stores numbers. The actions that can be carried out on strings are called string functions, and we shall look at, and illustrate, some of these string functions now.

```
10 INPUT"YOUR SURNAME,PLEASE";S$
20 INPUT"YOUR FORENAME,PLEASE";F$
30 PRINT F$+" "+S$;" ,THIS IS YOUR LIFE."
```

Fig. 3.4. Concatenating strings, using the + sign.

LEN, VAL and STR$

LEN and VAL are string functions which result in a number. Each has to be followed by a variable name of a string variable, enclosed in brackets. As you might expect, LEN gives the length of a string – its number of characters, and VAL gives the number value of a string

```
10 A$="TITLE"
20 A=LEN(A$)
30 TB=(20-A/2)
40 PRINTTAB(TB)A$
```

Fig. 3.5. Using LEN to centre a title.

which consists of a number in string form. Figure 3.5 shows LEN used to ensure that a title is printed centred on the screen. If we use any title of less than 40 letters, then by allocating this title to A$, it will be printed centred, so that it has the same margin on each side. The formula is the same as the one that we used in Chapter Two; all we have done here is to make use of LEN(A$) to find the number of characters in the string.

```
10 A$="12":B$="13"
20 PRINT A$+B$
30 PRINT VAL(A$)+VAL(B$)
```

Fig. 3.6. String-to-number conversion using VAL.

VAL is used when the string consists of digits, but stored in string form. What VAL does is to convert the string form back to a number form, so that we can carry out arithmetic. Figure 3.6 shows an example, in which A$ and B$ are string variables whose values are purely number values, with no letters present. If we simply use the + sign as in line 2$\emptyset$, then the result is joining, concatenation, of the strings, but if we convert each string to its number form using VAL, then we obtain the result we would expect from adding, the number 25.

When a string consists of a number and letters mixed, the use of VAL will extract only a number that is present at the start of the string. For example, if A$ = "25 Acacia Ave." then VAL(A$) = 25, but if A$ is assigned to "Route 12", then VAL(A$) = $\emptyset$. This is illustrated in Fig. 3.7, where the numbers are correctly extracted from A$ and B$, but not from C$ because when the computer starts to read the string it does not find a number.

```
10 A$="31ST.":B$="12 ACACIA AVE.":C$="JUL99Z"
20 PRINT"DAY NO. ";VAL(A$)
30 PRINT"HOUSE NO. ";VAL(B$)
40 PRINT"REG. NO. ";VAL(C$)
```

Fig. 3.7. Extracting numbers using VAL.

VAL is particularly useful when you have a program that requires you to make a choice from several numbered options (a 'menu'). If you use GET R$ to obtain the reply, then no matter what key has been pressed, the program will continue with no error messages. If you then want to extract a number, then VAL(R$) will get it; if a letter key was pressed, the value will be ∅. If some of your choices are of numbers and some are of letters, then by using VAL(R$) you can sort out the numbers, leaving you to check the letters if VAL(R$) is zero.

It's a good general principle that when your program uses an input from a user who may not be greatly skilled, then the computer must accept that input, and if it is wrong, show what is wrong with it. The REDO FROM START error message is useful when you know what causes it, but it is very much more satisfactory to be able to print something like:

YOU TYPED A LETTER – PLEASE TYPE A NUMBER
FROM THE CHOICE SHOWN

to remind the user of what is needed. We'll come back to that point later. For the moment, the important point is that the computer will accept any key, number or letter, as a value for R$ if you use GET R$, with no error message from the computer, and it is generally more satisfactory.

```
10 A=42:B=1.6
20 A$=STR$(A):B$=STR$(B)
30 PRINT A+B
40 PRINT A$+B$
50 C$=STR$(VAL(A$)+VAL(B$))
60 PRINT" C$ IS ";C$
```

Fig. 3.8. Converting numbers to string form using STR$.

The function STR$ is used to perform the opposite action to VAL(A$). Following STR$ there must be a number or number variable name, within brackets, and the action of STR$ will be to convert that number into string form. Figure 3.8 shows an example of this process in action. The numbers that are allocated to the number variables A and B in line 1∅ are converted into string form in line 2∅, using string variables A$ and B$. Those forms are different, as lines 3∅ and 4∅ show. We can add the numbers and then reconvert to string form by a line like 5∅ – I have deliberately used the string forms to illustrate the use of VAL. Finally, line 6∅ prints the value that is found by line 5∅, in string form.

Why should we want to put numbers into string form? The main reason is that strings can be manipulated in ways that numbers stored in the memory of the computer *in number form* cannot be. At this point, it's too early to see precisely what the advantages of using strings are, but all will become more clear as we go on. One point, however. When you convert a number to string form, as for example by using A = 3:A$ = STR$(A) then the length of the string is always one more than you might expect – it will be 2 in this example, for a single-digit number. The reason is that the STR$ action always leaves space for a sign in front of the number, + or −. If you don't put one there, then a blank space appears, and that's counted as a character by LEN.

CHR$ and ASC

When strings are stored, the computer has to convert each press of a key on the keyboard into a number code which represents a letter or digit, because all the computer can deal with is numbers. The standard number coding system that is used for this purpose is called ASCII code, from the initials of the American Standard Code for the Interchange of Information. The version of ASCII (we pronounce it as ASKEY) code numbers for each character of the 64 are illustrated in Appendix F of the manual. The character codes consist of numbers between 32, which is the space that you obtain by pressing the space-bar, and 127. The computer can also handle another set of codes which, on the 64 are reserved for graphics characters; the shapes that can be used for drawing pictures.

```
10 PRINT ASC("A")
20 PRINT ASC("2")
30 A$="COMMODORE"
40 X=ASC(A$)
50 PRINT X
```

Fig. 3.9. Finding ASC code numbers. Note that the 64 does not use the whole of the standard ASCII code set.

The instruction ASC(A$) will find the ASCII code for the first letter of the string A$. If there is only one letter, that's the one whose code is found. Since ASC(A$) by itself does not cause any output, we use it along with PRINT or X = to get the number code into a form we can use, as illustrated in Fig. 3.9. A line which contained just ASC(A$) would be rejected by the computer as a syntax error.

The CHR$(N) instruction performs the opposite action. Figure 3.10 shows a program in which the screen display changes from upper-case to lower-case on the screen. Since the 64 does not have separate codes for lower-case letters, unlike most computers, all of the letters on the screen are affected by the conversion. Line 1∅ clears the screen and prints the title, with line 2∅ used to create some space. When a (capital) letter is typed in line 3∅ and RETURN pressed, the use of code number 14 changes all the screen lettering to lower-case.

```
10 PRINT"⊐":PRINTTAB(16)"LETTERS"
20 PRINT:PRINT
30 INPUT"TYPE A CAPITAL LETTER,PLEASE";A$
40 A$=CHR$(14)+A$
50 PRINT"LOWER-CASE LETTER IS ";A$
```

Fig. 3.10. Using CHR$ to carry out the effect of a key.

String slicing

The most important actions that we can perform on strings, and only on strings, are the slicing actions. Slicing means selecting part of a string, perhaps the left-hand side, the right-hand side, or the middle. A slice of string can be printed or it can be allocated to another string. Figure 3.11 shows this in action, and will print your initials (two only) when given your surname and one forename. How is this done? Lines 1∅ to 3∅ should be familiar ground to you, and

```
10 PRINT"⊐":PRINT
20 INPUT"YOUR SURNAME,PLEASE";SN$
30 INPUT"YOUR FIRST NAME,PLEASE";FR$
40 A$=LEFT$(SN$,1)+"."
50 B$=LEFT$(FR$,1)+"."
60 PRINT"YOU WILL BE KNOWN AS ";B$+A$
```

Fig. 3.11. Using LEFT$ to extract part of a string.

they result in the two names being allocated to two different string variables, SN$ for the surname, and FR$ for the forename.

The processing starts in line 4∅. A new string, A$, is created, which consists of the first left-hand letter of SN$. This is done by using LEFT$(SN$,1) – one character from the left hand side of SN$. To this is joined (concatenated) a full-stop (period), which we add to show that the letter is an initial. This character needs to have quotes around it. Line 5∅ then does the same with FR$, and finally we run the two together in line 6∅, using another concatenation step.

This could have been done more economically if we had not been so intent on illustrating a principle. Suppose we had allocated a string variable name to the full stop (period) in line 15:

15 C$ = "."

then we could have ended our program at line 4∅ by making it read:

4∅ PRINT"YOU WILL BE KNOWN AS ";LEFT$(FR$,1)+C$+LEFT$(SN$,1)+C$

Alternatively, we could have programmed:

4∅ IN$=LEFT$(FR$,1)+C$+LEFT$(SN$,1)+C$

where IN$ (initial string) can be used anywhere else in the program – it's likely that your initials might be wanted more than once. This can be useful in games programs, where the initials of a player are given along with a score, or in business programs where someone who enters data into a file also enters initials as a check to trace errors.

If we use instructions such as S$ = LEFT$(NM$,J) then we can choose how many letters we slice from the string by allocating a value to J before the instruction to take the slice is executed. This can be used for some interesting effects, as we shall see later.

To take a character or a number of characters from the right hand side of a string, we use RIGHT$ (string name, number). Suppose, for example, that we have a set of components held in a store, with a code that is of the form XXX1234Q. The last letter indicates which row of shelves is used to store XXX, and the number of the part is 1234. We could print this shelf-row information by making use of RIGHT$, as indicated in Fig. 3.12. Once again, it's simple but useful.

```
10 PRINT"⬛":PRINT
20 READ CD$
30 PRINT"ITEM IS ON SHELF ";RIGHT$(CD$,1)
40 DATA PVJ417M
```

Fig. 3.12. Using RIGHT$ to find the right hand part of a string.

The most powerful of all the string slicing actions, however, is MID$. MID$ is followed, within brackets, by a string variable name and two numbers, each separated by commas. The sense is that the slice is taken from the character represented by the first number, and for as many characters as are represented by the second number.

Numbering, for this purpose, starts with 1, which is the first character on the left hand side of the string. As a formula, this is (string, start, how many).

For example, if we allocate A$ to "COMMODORE", then MID$(A$,4,3) is "MOD", because the fourth letter in COM-MODORE is M, and the three letters that start at this point are MOD. What makes the instruction so useful is the fact that we don't have to write numbers such as 4 and 3. We can, in their place, write number variables, such as J, K, or even expressions like $J*2-1$, or $K-5$ in place of the numbers. If you make the position number, the first one, too large, then nothing will be sliced. If you make the number of characters too large, then the slice will be taken to the end of the string.

```
10 PRINT"⌂":A$="COMMODORE"
20 X=INT(RND(1)*9)+1
30 Y=INT(RND(1)*8)+1
40 PRINT"RANDOM SELECTION IS ";MID$(A$,X,Y)
```

Fig. 3.13. How MID$ can extract letters from any part of a word.

Figure 3.13 shows a use of MID$ which is not exactly important, but which illustrates the use of the method. In line 1∅, A$ is allocated to COMMODORE and in lines 2∅ and 3∅ two random numbers are generated. The instruction RND(1) by itself will generate a number picked at random between ∅ and 1 but always more than ∅ and less than 1. Multiplying this random fraction by 9 will result in a number which must be greater than zero and less than 9. Add 1 to this, and you have a range of 1 to 9.999 (approximate). Take the INT of this lot, and the result is a whole number in the range of 1 to 9, chosen at random. Line 3∅ uses an almost identical formula to generate another random number lying between 1 and 8, and these numbers are then used in line 4∅ to pick a section at random from the string A$. You should obtain a different selection each time you run this program, showing that the numbers have indeed been picked at random.

Chapter Four
Decisions and Loops

Up to now, all the programs that we have used as examples have been linear programs. A linear program is one that carries out instructions in sequence, following the order of the line numbers of the program from start to finish. We can write a different type of step, a *branching* step that allows a program to proceed along different paths depending on the result of a test. The keyword to making a decision about branching is IF. 'IF' has to be followed by a test condition, and by the keyword THEN, followed in turn by what you want done if the test succeeds (the condition is true). An example will make it all clearer, I hope.

```
10 PRINT"J":PRINTTAB(10)"DECISIONS,DECISIONS"
20 PRINT:PRINT
30 INPUT"PLEASE TYPE YES OR NO";A$
40 IF LEFT$(A$,1)="Y"THEN PRINT"YOU TYPED YES":
GOTO 70
50 IF LEFT$(A$,1)="N"THEN PRINT "YOU TYPED NO":
GOTO70
60 PRINT"YOU CHEATED!"
70 END
```

Fig. 4.1. Using IF to make decision steps.

Figure 4.1 shows a program that allows the computer to act differently according to your answers, YES or NO, to a question. In line 4Ø, the first letter of the answer is compared to the letter Y. If the two match, the phrase YOU TYPED YES is printed, and a new command GOTO 7Ø causes the next line of the program to be line 7Ø (the end), not line 5Ø. If the reply was NO then line 4Ø is *not* executed, and the next line, line 5Ø, is tried. In line 5Ø, if the first letter of your answer word was N, then the phrase that is printed is YOU TYPED NO and once again the program moves to line 7Ø, the end. If what you answered matches with neither YES nor NO, then line 6∅ is executed, and the program ends, as before, in line 7∅.

It's a trivial example, but it indicates how a decision can be made among three possibilities (Y, N, or anything else), and can cause different effects. In most 'real' programs, the action that is carried out when the test succeeds is not just a print action. We can, for example, use:

THEN GOTO 1∅∅∅

following a test. This means that if the test succeeds, the next line that will be carried out will be line 1∅∅∅, and the program will then run from this line onward (lines 1∅1∅,1∅2∅ ... etc.). In this way, you can direct the computer to do much more than a simple PRINT or other one-step instruction as the result of a test.

Note that anything which follows the IF ... will be ignored when the test does *not* succeed. This includes following statements of a multi-statement line. If, for example, you have a line like:

1∅∅ IF Y = 2 THEN GOTO 2∅∅:PRINT"CHEAT!":GOTO5∅

then the instructions PRINT"CHEAT!":GOTO5∅ are never carried out for any value of Y. It is generally easier to understand IF tests when each one is put on a separate line. This ensures that if one test fails, the next one will be tried, and we can use GOTO after each IF test to make sure that the program moves to the correct line when a test succeeds. Remember that when a test fails, the next line that will be executed will be the next line in number order.

GOTO and GOSUB

The IF ... THEN decision test can be used to alter the 'flow' of a program, meaning that it alters the sequence of lines that are carried out. GOTO and GOSUB are commands that are also closely associated with the flow of programs, because these commands direct the program to the next line that will be executed. When you program a line like:

2∅ GOTO 1∅∅∅
3∅ PRINT A

you force the flow of the program to move from line 2∅ to line 1∅∅∅ in place of line 3∅. There is nothing in the use of GOTO 1∅∅∅ that will cause the program to return to line 3∅, however. By contrast:

2∅ GOSUB 1∅∅∅
3∅ PRINT A

will cause a branch at line 2∅, but the program will return later to line 3∅. GOSUB is a shortened version of GO to SUBroutine, and a subroutine is a piece of program, one line or more, which can be executed out of line number sequence. The distinguishing feature of a subroutine is that it will return the program to the instruction following the one that caused the branch. In the example above, then, control will return to line 3∅. If we had:

1∅∅ GOSUB 1∅∅∅: PRINT "DONE"

then when the subroutine returned, the PRINT action would be carried out because even the next statement of a multi-statement line will be carried out after a GOSUB.

```
10 PRINT"⊐":PRINTTAB(15)"SUBROUTINE"
20 PRINT"THIS IS A";
30 GOSUB1000
40 PRINT" SUBROUTINE"
50 PRINT"MIX GREEN LIGHT AND BLUE LIGHT"
60 PRINT" AND GET - ";
70 GOSUB1000
80 PRINT" LIGHT"
90 END
1000 PRINT " YELLOW";
1010 RETURN
```

Fig. 4.2. How a subroutine is used.

To illustrate this, take a look at the example in Fig. 4.2. Silly it may be, but it does show what a subroutine does and how it is programmed. The subroutine in line 1∅∅∅ prints the word YELLOW, with a semicolon placed after it to ensure that the next PRINT instruction does *not* cause a new line to be printed. The point here is that the word RETURN in line 1∅1∅ will cause the program to do just that – to return to the instruction following the GOSUB that caused the subroutine to run. The flow of the program of Fig. 4.2, using line numbers to trace the action, will be 1∅, 2∅, 3∅, 1∅∅∅, 1∅1∅, 4∅, 5∅, 6∅, 7∅, 1∅∅∅, 1∅1∅, 8∅, 9∅. By using END in line 9∅, we prevent the program from continuing from line 8∅ to line 1∅∅∅, and so printing YELLOW once again. An unwanted use of a subroutine like this is called 'crashing through', and the use of END makes certain that the subroutine is used only when it is 'called' by the use of GOSUB1ØØØ. If you forget to use RETURN at the end of the subroutine, your program will end at line 1ØØØ when the subroutine is first called. If you forget the END in line 9Ø, then the program will print YELLOW at the end, and you will get the error message RETURN WITHOUT GOSUB – a sure sign of a crash through.

```
10 INPUT"YOUR TITLE, PLEASE";TT$
20 PRINT"□":PRINT:GOSUB1000
30 END
1000 LN=LEN(TT$):TB=20-LN/2
1010 PRINTTAB(TB)TT$
1020 RETURN
```

Fig. 4.3. A title-centring subroutine.

Notice that the same subroutine can be called from more than one place in the program. This is what makes the subroutine so useful – it can be used more than once and for more than one purpose. Just to drive this point home, Fig. 4.3 shows a subroutine which will print a title TT$ centred on the screen. The title should not contain more

```
10 PRINT"□"
20 TT$="THIS IS A TITLE WHICH"
30 GOSUB1000
40 TT$="IS MUCH LONGER THAN NORMAL"
50 GOSUB 1000
60 END
1000 LN=LEN(TT$):TB=20-LN/2
1010 PRINTTAB(TB)TT$
1020 RETURN
```

Fig. 4.4. Why the subroutine is so useful.

than 38 letters, but providing it is suitable it will be printed centred on the line that we select. Suppose you have a title of more than 38 letters? The use of the subroutine makes this easy, as Fig. 4.4 shows – if you add lines 1Ø to 6Ø to the subroutine, then the title will be printed in two sections, with each section centred on its print line.

Looping lines

GOTO and GOSUB can cause a program to branch in the way that we have demonstrated, but there is another very important type of branch, called a loop, which can be achieved by using GOTO. If a program includes a GOTO which is followed by a line number that is *lower* than the number of the line that contains the GOTO, then a set of lines will be repeated until something happens to stop the repetition. The 'something' will usually be an IF test which may use

```
10 PRINT"⬛":TT$="ACCUMULATIONS":GOSUB1000
20 N=0
30 PRINT"TYPE A NUMBER, PLEASE";
40 INPUT J:N=N+J
50 PRINT"RUNNING TOTAL IS ";N
60 GOTO30
1000 LN=LEN(TT$):TB=20-LN/2
1010 PRINTTAB(TB)TT$
1020 PRINT:PRINT:RETURN
```

Fig. 4.5. A running-total program. You may need to use RESTORE with RUN/STOP to break out of this one.

another GOTO, or be a part of the original GOTO. Figure 4.5 shows a running-total program which has no method of escape – to stop this running you will have to use the RESTORE and STOP keys. We can make the program break out of its loop by adding a couple of lines:

45 IF J=∅ THEN GOTO 7∅
7∅ END

With these lines added, if you enter a zero, the program will stop looping back to line 3∅ and will end at line 7∅ instead. A better use of the IF test is to *cause* the loop to return, so that the program ends

```
10 PRINT"⬛":TT$="ACCUMULATIONS":GOSUB1000
20 N=0
30 PRINT"TYPE A NUMBER, PLEASE";
40 INPUT J:N=N+J
50 PRINT"RUNNING TOTAL IS ";N
60 IF J<>0 THEN GOTO 30
70 END
1000 LN=LEN(TT$):TB=20-LN/2
1010 PRINTTAB(TB)TT$
1020 PRINT:PRINT:RETURN
```

Fig. 4.6. Altering the running-total program so that entry of ∅ will stop the program.

when the test fails. This requires only one GOTO, and looks neater, as Fig. 4.6 illustrates.

Conditions

So far, the only condition that we have used to any extent in the IF test has been the test of equality; more precisely, identity, using the = sign. We can also test to find if items are unequal, or if one is greater than another. Figure. 4.7 shows some of the other conditions that

---

=	Equal to (must be *identical* for this to succeed)
>	Greater than (left side greater than right side)
<	Less than (left side less than right side)
<>	Not equal
>=	Greater than or equal
<=	Less than or equal

These Can be Used With

AND	Several quantities tested
OR	Any one of a group tested
NOT	Test for opposite

Fig. 4.7. The conditions that can be tested, and the signs that are used.

can be tested, either for numbers or for strings. When numbers are tested, some care is needed to ensure that the test is not spoiled by errors (Fig. 4.8) caused by the way in which numbers are stored (see Chapter Two). The numbers should always be rounded off to the

```
10 A=2.7:B=2.6
20 C=9:D=90
30 IFA-B=C/DTHEN PRINT"EQUAL":END
40 PRINTA-B;" IS NOT EQUAL TO ";C/D
```

Fig. 4.8. The effect of errors on stored numbers.

same number of decimal places before they are tested for equality. When strings are tested, the basis for comparison is the ASCII code numbers, starting with the first letter of each string. Since the ASCII code for T is greater than the code for S, then 'S' is regarded as a string which is less than the string 'T'. If the first letters of two strings are identical, the second letters are compared, and so on, so that the word ELECTRIC is considered as coming lower in a list than ELECTRON, because 'I' comes earlier than 'O' and has a lower ASCII code. Figure 4.9 illustrates this in action – two words can be

```
10 PRINTCHR$(147):TT$="ALPHABETICAL SORT":CC$=
"ORDER IS- "
20 GOSUB1000
30 INPUT"FIRST WORD";A$
40 INPUT"SECOND WORD";B$
50 IF A$<B$ THEN PRINT CC$;A$;" THEN ";B$:
GOTO70
60 PRINT CC$;B$;" THEN ";A$
70 END
1000 LN=LEN(TT$):TB=20-LN/2
1010 PRINTTAB(TB)TT$
1020 RETURN
```

Fig. 4.9. Comparing strings on the basis of alphabetical order.

typed, and the program will tell you which is the correct alphabetical order. This is a very simple example, and normally when we want to arrange items into alphabetical order we need something much more elaborate – more of that later.

FOR ... NEXT

Looping is such an important process that a special set of loop instructions has been devised, avoiding the use of GOTO. The general form of the loop is that it starts with:

FOR variable = number TO number

in which we have to fill in values for a pair of numbers, and use a variable name. We can also use variable names in place of the numbers, or even use expressions like $K \uparrow 2 - 5$. The loop returns at a stage in the program (later) which contains the word NEXT.

As usual, an example is more helpful than a description, and Fig. 4.10 shows an elementary example which will print a phrase ten times. Line 3∅ sets up the number of repetitions by setting a variable N to start at 1 and to increase by a step of 1 each time the loop is used, until the value of N exceeds 1∅. For as long as the value of N is 1∅ or less, the loop will be carried out, but when N exceeds 1∅, the loop stops, and the next instruction to be obeyed is in line 6∅, the

```
10 PRINTCHR$(147):TT$="FOR-NEXT LOOP"
20 GOSUB1000
30 FOR N=1 TO 10
40 PRINT"COMMODORE 64 COMPUTING"
50 NEXT
60 PRINT"END OF LOOP"
70 END
1000 LN=LEN(TT$):TB=20-LN/2
1010 PRINTTAB(TB)TT$
1020 RETURN
```

Fig. 4.10. Using the FOR ... NEXT loop.

instruction following NEXT. This applies also if NEXT is in a multi-statement line, and if the FOR N = 1 TO 1∅ is also in a multi-statement line. The value of N when the loop stops will always be one step greater than the maximum value that you specified, so that in Fig. 4.10, N will have a value of 11 when the program ends.

You can, if you like, repeat the name of the variable following NEXT, so that it reads NEXT N (or NEXTN). This is optional, but it can be useful in a program that contains a lot of steps in the loop, so that you know which loop is being terminated at that point. If you don't specify any step size, this quantity is always set at 1, but if you add to the FOR ... NEXT part of the loop the additional instruction STEP, you can control the step size for yourself. For example, you could use:

FOR N = 1 TO 5 STEP .25   to step in units of one quarter,

or:

FOR N = 1∅∅ TO ∅ STEP −1   to obtain a countdown.

Uses of loops

Loops can be used for counting, for timing and for repeating operations. Take a look at some examples of these operations in action. Figure. 4.11 illustrates how items can be counted out from a DATA line by using the READ controlled by a FOR ... NEXT loop. So that the program runs one step at a time, lines 7∅ and 8∅ have been put in to ensure that the NEXT instruction is not obeyed until a key has been pressed. If you keep your finger on the RETURN key for too long when the program starts, though, it will print out all of the values. To avoid this, a time loop has been set up

```
10 PRINTCHR$(147):TT$="ITEM COUNT"
20 GOSUB1000
30 FOR N=1TO1000:NEXT
40 FOR N=1TO10
50 READ A$
60 PRINT"ITEM ";N;" IS ";A$
70 PRINT"PRESS ANY KEY TO PROCEED"
80 GETZ$:IF Z$="" THEN 80
90 NEXT
100 END
110 DATABULLDOG,BEAR,EAGLE,DINGO,GOOSE,SWAN,
WOLF,FOX,DUCK,ANTELOPE
1000 LN=LEN(TT$):TB=20-LN/2
1010 PRINTTAB(TB)TT$
1020 RETURN
```

Fig. 4.11. Using a FOR ... NEXT loop to control a READ ... DATA program.

in line 3∅. This simply allows a time delay between lines 2∅ and 4∅, and the time that is needed is set by the speed of operation of the 64. With a number of 1∅∅∅ as shown, the time delay is approximately 1½ seconds.

```
10 PRINTCHR$(147):TT$="WORDS!":GOSUB1000
20 INPUT"STARTING WORD";A$
30 L=LEN(A$):W$=""
40 FOR J=1 TO 10
50 LN=INT(RND(1)*(L-2)+2)
60 FOR N=1 TO LN
70 SR=INT(RND(1)*L+1)
80 W$=W$+MID$(A$,SR,1)
90 NEXT
100 PRINT W$:W$=""
110 NEXT
120 END
1000 LN=LEN(TT$):TB=20-LN/2
1010 PRINTTAB(TB)TT$
1020 RETURN
```

Fig. 4.12. Randomly generated 'words' picked out from a starting word.

This program has illustrated two uses of the FOR ... NEXT loop, but the next illustration is much more elaborate. This one (Fig. 4.12) uses FOR ... NEXT loops to generate groups of ten 'words' with letters selected at random from a starting word. The title of the program is printed as usual, and the starting word is requested. If the starting word is reasonably long, then a large number of 'words' can be created from it by this process – this is a useful way of finding names for your 'aliens'! The length of the starting word is found in line 3∅, and the string that will be used to accumulate letters into a word, W$, is set to a blank, " ". The loop that starts in line 4∅ determines the number of these 'words' that will be generated and at the start of each one, the quantity LN, the length of the word, is calculated. It will be a random length which must not exceed L and which must not be less than 2. Each word of a group of ten is then created by the loop that starts in line 6∅. This uses LN as its finishing value, and picks letters from A$ at random, using SR as the starting point for each letter. The word builds up because of line 8∅, which adds to W$ each letter as it is picked out, and calls the result by the same variable name of W$. This loop ends in line 9∅, and the word is printed in line 1∅∅. The variable W$ is then reset to a blank (otherwise more will be added to it), so that it is ready to accumulate another set of letters when the NEXT in line 11∅ is executed. We could have used the variable names with each NEXT, so that we had NEXT N in line 9∅ and NEXT J in line 11∅ so as to remind us of the correct order – each loop must end in the reverse order of starting. If you start with:

FOR N = 1 TO 1∅ : FOR J = 1 TO 5

then you must finish with NEXT J:NEXT N. The 'inner' loop, using J, must be complete before the outer loop, using N, can be completed. If you simply use NEXT, the computer will take care of this for you, but if you specify the variable names, then you must get them in the correct order. This use of one loop inside another is called 'nesting', and each loop that is contained inside another one must be completely contained, with its start and finish points within the outer loop. If your nesting goes wrong, your chickens will come home to roost in the form of a NEXT WITHOUT FOR error message. Another important point about loops is that the counting variables, such as N, J in these examples, must *not* be re-assigned to any other number while the loop is running. This could end the loop prematurely, or possibly prevent it from ever ending! One exception is when we read a value that is tested and when a value is read that must end the loop, the counter variable is set to the end value. This would use a line such as:

IF A$ = "END" THEN N = 1∅∅

if the loop started with FOR N = 1 TO 1ØØ.

Subscripted variables

So far, when we have used items read from a list, we have used one, printed it, and then re-allocated the variable name to another item. You can't do this if you need to make use of all of the items in a list. If you want to add a set of figures in an accounts program, for example, you still need to be able to use the individual figures when you display the items. To get around this problem, computers use what are called subscripted variables.

A subscripted variable means one with a number-tag attached. Suppose we choose a number variable such as A. Instead of using other variable names like B,C,D, ... for other numbers, we can use A(1), A(2), A(3), ..., pronounced as A-of-1, A-of-2, A-of-3, ... and so on. Each of these will be treated separately as a different variable name with a different value. What makes the scheme so useful is that the subscript numbers within the brackets can themselves be represented by another number variable.

```
10 PRINTCHR$(147):TT$="SUBSCRIPTS":GOSUB1000
20 FOR N=1 TO 10
30 READ A(N)
40 NEXT
50 INPUT"PICK A NUMBER, 1 TO 10";X
60 IF X>10 OR X<1 THEN PRINT "INCORRECT RANGE":
GOTO50
70 PRINT"ITEM CHOICE IS ";A(X)
80 GOTO50
90 END
100 DATA105.6,112,27,93,106,54,22,1.76,9.21,
1174.2
120 END
1000 LN=LEN(TT$):TB=20-LN/2
1010 PRINTTAB(TB)TT$
1020 RETURN
```

Fig. 4.13. Using an array – this is a number array.

Take a look, for example, at Fig. 4.13. This reads a set of numbers from a DATA list into a set of subscripted variable names. This set of subscripted variables is called an array, so what we have present after line 4Ø has been executed is a number array. In lines 5Ø to 8Ø, we choose a number between 1 and 1∅, and the program prints the corresponding value that exists in the array. If we choose number 3, for example, then A(3), which is 27, is printed out. Note the use of line 6∅ to reject impossible choices of array subscript numbers – this type of line is called a 'mugtrap'. The use of a mugtrap, or several mugtraps, is essential if the program is to be used by unskilled operators. Even when you have designed a program for yourself and use it yourself, you'll be grateful at times for the use of a good mugtrap to save you from your own mistakes!

```
10 PRINTCHR$(147):TT$="STRING ARRAY":GOSUB1000
20 FOR N=1TO10:PRINT"ENTER NAMES, PLEASE"
30 PRINT"ITEM ";N;" PLEASE";
40 INPUT WD$(N)
50 NEXT
60 PRINTCHR$(147):TT$="RANDOM CHOICE":GOSUB1000
70 PRINT"EACH TIME YOU PRESS A KEY YOU WILL GET"
80 PRINT"AN ITEM CHOSEN AT RANDOM."
90 PRINT" START NOW....TO END, PRESS 'Q'"
100 GET A$:IF A$="" THEN 100
110 J=INT(RND(1)*10+1)
120 PRINT WD$(J)
130 IF A$<>"Q" THEN 100
140 END
1000 PRINTTAB(20-(LEN(TT$))/2)TT$:RETURN
```

Fig. 4.14. Using a string array, with values inserted by a FOR ... NEXT loop using an INPUT instruction in the loop.

We have illustrated the use of a number array which was created by using the READ ... DATA instruction in a loop, but we can equally easily use string arrays, and fill them either from READ ... DATA or by the use of INPUT lines. Figure 4.14 shows an example of a string array filled from an INPUT statement. The program allows you to input a number of string items such as names, and then makes random choices. You could make it the basis of a 'what-shall-I-read/listen-to/do' sort of choice, or if you happen to be Chancellor of the Exchequer, a 'what-*could*-I-do' choice. Most of the program should be familiar material to you, but note the use of line 13∅, which looks for the decision to quit. If the Q key was *not* pressed in line 1∅∅, then this test in line 13∅ will cause the program to loop back to line 1∅∅ to pick again at random. If the Q key was pressed, however, the program ends in line 14∅.

Dimensioning

In these examples, we have used arrays which were of only ten items. This is the maximum number that the computer will accept without notice, as it were. Arrays take up quite a lot of storage space in the memory, and space is allocated for subscript numbers up to 10 only when you switch the computer on, so that if you want to use larger arrays, you have to reserve the space. This is done very early in the program by using an instruction called DIM. DIM means DIMension, and the dimension of an array is the maximum size of subscript number that you will want to use. Suppose, for example, that you are writing a program for cataloguing film slides, and that you have 1000 titles to list. If you choose the variable name of SLIDE$ (yes, you can use variable names of more than two letters, but the computer ignores all but the first two), then the dimension instruction must be:

10 DIM SLIDE$(1000)

or

10 DIM SL$(1000)

and this will reserve the use of subscripts of up to 1000 for this variable. If you try to exceed this number, you will get a BAD SUBSCRIPT error message.

When you dimension an array, for example N$(100), for a hundred items, this does not dimension any other arrays, only the array with that variable name. Every array that uses a number greater than 10 must be dimensioned, and the BASIC of the 64 allows you to carry out the dimensioning of a set of arrays together. You could, for example, have:

10 DIM ITEM$(100), NT (100), CN(50), HD$(50)

to dimension four sets of arrays, two with dimensions of 100 and two with 50.

Once you have dimensioned an array, you must not attempt to alter that dimensioning again in the course of the program. This is because once the computer has allocated memory for an array (strictly speaking, for the subscripts of the array), it will have used the memory above and below this region for other purposes. A change of use will therefore mean having to spring-clean the memory, and re-allocate it, and this can't be done while a program is using the memory. Any attempt to re-dimension an array will therefore cause the error message: REDIM'D ARRAY

Matrices

The 64 allows you to set up arrays with more than one dimension, a variety that we call a matrix (one matrix, two matrices). The word is also used for a criss-cross grid arrangement, a way of writing number relationships, and a management system in which you have two bosses and don't need to pay any attention to either of them. In our use of the word 'matrix', however, it simply means a set of items that belong together and which can be given one variable name.

The simplest matrix to understand is the two-dimensional matrix. Suppose that we are keeping a track of the articles on the 64 in our favourite magazines. You would need, at least, to keep a record of the name of the article and the name of the magazine. If we allocated the variable AR$ for the article name, and MG$ for the magazine, we could use two arrays to hold the names, but since the items belong together, we could use a matrix called AR$(X,Y). The meaning of this is most easily seen if we look at the items of this matrix (Fig. 4.15). Supposing that item 1 is an article, then the variable name for this article is AR$(1,1), and the name of the magazine is AR$(1,2). The next entry, item 2, would use AR$(2,1) for the article name, and AR$(2,2) for the magazine name. The system is that the first number is the item number, and the second is the classification – article or magazine.

ROWS ↓	1	COLUMNS 2
1.	programming	*Byte*
2.	machine code	*P.C.W.*
3.	Commodore hints	*Kilobaud*

(as many rows of items as you need)

The matrix is always written as (row, column)
so that *Kilobaud* would be item (3,2)

Fig. 4.15. The row-column representation of a matrix.

A matrix is used when the components of each item belong tightly together, and are never going to be re-allocated. For example, if we want to arrange our articles in alphabetical order, we shall want the correct magazine names still associated with the articles. We are not likely to want a list which has the magazine names also put into alphabetical order so that the article called *Beating The Opposition* is associated with the magazine *Byte* when it actually appeared in *Popular Computing*!

We needn't stop at article name and magazine name, of course; we could have year and month of issue, and the page number also listed. Suppose we have a program which will search for a given article name, and will then place on to the screen the name of the magazine, the year and month of issue, and the page at which the article starts. We might then have, for article 1, the variable name AR$(1,1) for the name of the article, AR$(1,2) for the magazine name, AR$(1,3) for the year and month, and AR$(1,4) for the page number. Our matrix would now consist of four columns and as many rows as we have articles to list. A matrix like this needs a dimension statement of DIM AR$(1ØØ,4) if you want to store 100 items in it. One dimension is for the number of rows, the other for the number of columns. This is the simplest way to visualise a two-dimensional matrix – as a set of rows and columns.

If we have a set of items that are related to both row and column items, then we could create a three-dimensional matrix, which we might dimension, for example, by DIM TD$(1ØØ,4,2). It's unusual to need so many dimensions for a simple catalogue program, but you might need to go to three-dimensional (or even more) matrices for programs of the financial spreadsheet type, or games programs of the 'adventure' type.

Number matrices are used for the solution of certain types of mathematical problems. In general, unless you understand the mathematical theory, you are unlikely to be able to make much use of number matrices. For that reason, there is little point in discussing them in this book.

Chapter Five
Data Processing and Program Design

Data processing is the task that computers were designed for in the first place, and for which most computer owners have some need. The simple machines that are designed primarily for games purposes are generally poorly equipped for data processing, but the 64 as you might by now expect, is fully able to carry out this important work as well. This chapter will deal with data processing actions, and how programs are designed.

A data processing program will normally make provision for entry of data, like article names and pages, the recording of the data on tape or on disk and recovery of previously recorded data, processing and display. Processing may mean arranging into alphabetical order, picking out a specified item, adding amounts for a given year, counting how many entries concern a requested topic, and so on. Display may mean using the screen, but is much more likely to require the printer to turn out a permanent record on paper. Data processing is the main activity of any computer that is used for business purposes.

You might think that the very wide variety of tasks that the computer could be called on to do might make it impossible to say much of a general nature on this subject. You would be wrong, because all data processing programs are surprisingly similar. In addition, the best ways of designing a program in BASIC apply with the same force whether the program is intended for data processing or for any other purpose. One feature that is common to practically all data processing programs, however, is the use of a menu.

A menu, as the name suggests, is a method of presenting a set of choices for the user. The program should be devised so that it always returns to this menu after a task, selected from the menu, has been completed. In this way, the user will be able to carry out a set of different activities on the data that is already stored in the computer, without having to re-load any information. This implies that the

```
100 PRINT"⬛":TT$="MENU":GOSUB1000
110 PRINTTAB(2)"1. ENTER NAMES."
120 PRINTTAB(2)"2. RECORD ITEMS."
130 PRINTTAB(2)"3. REPLAY PREVIOUS LIST."
140 PRINTTAB(2)"4. UPDATE PREVIOUS LIST."
150 PRINTTAB(2)"5. SELECT ITEM."
160 PRINTTAB(2)"6. END PROGRAM."
170 PRINT"PRESS NUMBER KEY TO SELECT."
180 GETA$:IF A$=""THEN180
190 V=VAL(A$):IF V=1THEN1500
200 IF V=2 THEN 2000
210 IF V=3 THEN 2500
220 IF V=4 THEN 3000
230 IF V=5 THEN 3500
240 IF V=6 THEN END
250 PRINT"⬛":PRINT"YOUR ANSWER ";A$;" IS NOT
UNDERSTOOD."
260 PRINT"PLEASE TRY AGAIN":GOTO110
1000 PRINTTAB(20-LEN(TT$)/2)TT$:RETURN
1500 PRINT"ROUTINE 1":END
2000 PRINT"ROUTINE 2.":END
2500 PRINT"ROUTINE 3.":END
3000 PRINT"ROUTINE 4.":END
3500 PRINT"ROUTINE 5.":END
```

Fig. 5.1. A menu which can form the core of a data processing program.

menu should always contain a 'quit' option, the selection of which will end the program.

One simple way of organising a menu is illustrated in Fig. 5.1. Each choice is listed, along with a reference number, and the user is requested to make the choice by pressing the appropriate number key. This is done by using GET A$ in line 18$\emptyset$, with a string variable used so that any key is acceptable. The value is then found from V = VAL(A$), and tested in lines 19$\emptyset$ to 24$\emptyset$ to direct the program to the correct routines. If a wrong key has been pressed, the program will reach lines 25$\emptyset$, 26$\emptyset$, so that the message is printed, and the program returns to the menu display. Each routine that is used, shown in this example as starting at line numbers 15$\emptyset\emptyset$, 2$\emptyset\emptyset\emptyset$, etc., should end with an END, so that the program is completed after each selection. An alternative would be to end with GOTO 1$\emptyset\emptyset$ to repeat the menu.

The BASIC of the 64 allows several variations on this theme. One of these is illustrated in Fig. 5.2, making use of the ON N GOTO instruction. In this instruction, N is a number variable which is used

```
100 PRINT"⊐":TT$="MENU":GOSUB1000
110 PRINTTAB(2)"1. ENTER NAMES."
120 PRINTTAB(2)"2. RECORD ITEMS."
130 PRINTTAB(2)"3. REPLAY PREVIOUS LIST."
140 PRINTTAB(2)"4. UPDATE PREVIOUS LIST."
150 PRINTTAB(2)"5. SELECT ITEM."
160 PRINTTAB(2)"6. END PROGRAM."
170 PRINT"PRESS NUMBER KEY TO SELECT."
180 GETA$:IF A$=""THEN180
190 V=VAL(A$):IFV<1 OR V>6 THEN250
200 ON V GOTO 1500,2000,2500,3000,3500,4000
210 GOTO4000
250 PRINT"⊐":PRINT"YOUR ANSWER ";A$;" IS NOT
UNDERSTOOD."
260 PRINT"PLEASE TRY AGAIN":GOTO110
1000 PRINTTAB(20-LEN(TT$)/2)TT$:RETURN
1500 PRINT"ROUTINE 1":END
2000 PRINT"ROUTINE 2.":END
2500 PRINT"ROUTINE 3.":END
3000 PRINT"ROUTINE 4.":END
3500 PRINT"ROUTINE 5.":END
4000 END
```

Fig. 5.2. Using the ON N GOTO instruction for a menu.

for the user choice – we have used V for this variable in Fig. 5.2. The value of this variable is used to make a selection from a list of line numbers which follow the GOTO part of the instruction. If V is 3, for example, the GOTO will take the line number which is third in the list of line numbers. Figure 5.2 shows this in action, replacing lines 19∅ to 24∅ of the program in Fig. 5.1. When this method is used, the program will need a test of the number that the user entered *before* the use of ON V GOTO. This will have to ensure that the value of V is reasonable – not less than 1, not more than 6, and with no fractions or negative signs. If an incorrect number reaches the ON V GOTO line, then the error message UNDEF'D STATEMENT will appear. A suitable mugtrap for faulty numbers is illustrated in Fig. 5.2, line 19∅.

There is also the instruction ON N GOSUB, and this has benefits both for program operation and also for the way in which programs can be designed. Figure 5.3 shows how a menu choice is arranged when this method is used – the advantage here is that we do not need a GOTO1∅∅ instruction at the end of each of the subroutines that deal with the menu choices, simply a RETURN on all except the

```
100 PRINT"⬛":TT$="MENU":GOSUB1000
110 PRINTTAB(2)"1. ENTER NAMES."
120 PRINTTAB(2)"2. RECORD ITEMS."
130 PRINTTAB(2)"3. REPLAY PREVIOUS LIST."
140 PRINTTAB(2)"4. UPDATE PREVIOUS LIST."
150 PRINTTAB(2)"5. SELECT ITEM."
160 PRINTTAB(2)"6. END PROGRAM."
170 PRINT"PRESS NUMBER KEY TO SELECT."
180 GETA$:IF A$=""THEN180
190 V=VAL(A$):IFV<1 OR V>6 THEN250
200 ON V GOSUB 1500,2000,2500,3000,3500,4000
210 GOTO4000
250 PRINT"⬛":PRINT"YOUR ANSWER ";A$;" IS NOT
UNDERSTOOD."
260 PRINT"PLEASE TRY AGAIN":GOTO110
1000 PRINTTAB(20-LEN(TT$)/2)TT$:RETURN
1500 PRINT"ROUTINE 1.":RETURN
2000 PRINT"ROUTINE 2.":RETURN
2500 PRINT"ROUTINE 3.":RETURN
3000 PRINT"ROUTINE 4.":RETURN
3500 PRINT"ROUTINE 5.":RETURN
4000 END
```

Fig. 5.3. Using ON N GOSUB. In all of these examples, it would be preferable to use an integer for the variable (ON N% GOSUB for example).

"END PROGRAM" choice. When any other subroutine ends, the program will return to line 2∅∅, which directs control to line 21∅. This makes the 'flow' of the program clearer, because anyone reading the program can now see how the menu return is arranged, instead of having to check for a GOTO at the end of each of the routines that are selected from the menu.

Figure 5.4 shows a much more visual type of menu arrangement in which the choices are not numbered, but are arranged on separate lines. The choice is made by moving an arrow which is in turn controlled by arrowed ↑↓ cursor keys, and then pressing the spacebar when the arrow is pointing to the choice that you want. This avoids the possibility of an incorrect selection, because the program controls the movement of the arrow within the limits of the number of lines on the screen. It also allows easier selection from a large number of items, because GET A$ is usable only if the reply can be a single key (though you still have the choice of letters as well as numbers). A pictorial menu of this type is sometimes more appropriate for programs than the choose-a-number type.

```
10 PRINT"⊐":PRINT:PRINT
20 AD=1104:N=1:CL=55376
100 PRINTTAB(2)"1. FIRST."
110 PRINTTAB(2)"2. SECOND."
120 PRINTTAB(2)"3. THIRD."
140 PRINT:PRINT
150 POKEAD+40*N,62:POKECL+40*N,7
160 GET A$:IF A$=""THEN160
170 V=ASC(A$)
175 POKEAD+40*N,32
180 IF V=17THEN N=N+1
190 IF V=145 THEN N=N-1
200 IF N=4THEN N=1
210 IF N=0 THEN N=3
220 IF V<>32 THEN 150
230 ON N GOSUB 1000,2000,3000
240 END
1000 PRINT"1ST.":RETURN
2000 PRINT"2ND.":RETURN
3000 PRINT"3RD.":RETURN
```

Fig. 5.4. A visual choice menu. Moving the marker to the selected position and pressing the space-bar makes the choice. See Chapter Six for an explanation of the POKE instruction.

Program design

The use of a program based on a menu, with subroutines to carry out the actions that are specified by menu selection, is the key to simple program design for data processing. The difficult part of designing a program is not the use of the programming language, it is the analysis of the problem that you want to solve into steps that can be put into the form of program subroutines. By designing your programs 'top-down', this analysis can be made much easier. Top-down means that you start by considering the outline of the problem only, and then gradually work down to finer details. For most data processing problems, design will therefore start with considering:

(1) what type of data is being dealt with,
(2) whether recording and replay of data is needed,
(3) whether printed copy is needed,
(4) whether recorded data needs to be updated,
(5) what you expect to see on the screen or have to type on the keyboard at each stage in the program.

Unless your requirements are unusually complex, it should be possible to make these decisions and write them down early in the design process. Writing the specification is vitally important, because it is surprisingly easy to lose sight of your objectives later on when you start to program the details. The more paper you use at the planning stage, the more likely it is that your program will run correctly.

The next step is to design the menu choices. At this stage, remember that each action will return to the menu, so only the most important choices need to be included. If there is a step which is only ever used as part of another one, it need not appear in the menu. For example, if data is *always* to be alphabetically sorted after entry, there is no point in having a menu choice of SORT DATA ITEMS. Take time over your menu, because the appearance of the menu and the choice that it presents can make all the difference between a program that will be a pleasure to use and one which gives you very little satisfaction, or even perhaps one you try to avoid using. Once the menu is designed, the main part of program planning is finished!

The 'core' of the program can now be written. Start writing the menu section, starting at line 1∅∅ so that you have ample space for dimensioning instructions and other routines in lines 1 to 99. Whether you use ON N GOSUB or a set of lines such as:

IF V% = 1 THEN GOSUB

it is always an advantage to use GOSUB rather than GOTO, because the RETURN at the end of the GOSUB will always lead to the next line of the menu. This makes your program simple to follow – something for which you will be grateful as you extend the program, and which will be even more useful if you have to revise, amend or extend it later.

This completes a skeleton around which your program can be constructed. As it happens, this skeleton can probably be used for many other programs so that it is a good idea to save this core program on tape or disk, ready to load in next time you want to devise a program. The important point is what you have done so far avoids the type of detail that will cramp your style later. Each action of the program is now dealt with using subroutines, and each one of these subroutines can now be designed as if it were a little program in its own right. What you now have to do is to decide the order of importance of the subroutines, what variables they will use, and what values need to be passed from one subroutine to another. One important point here is that none of the subroutines must use the variable name that has been used to select items from the menu (we used V in our example). In our example, if V = 2 is selected so as to start the second subroutine, which might be one that reads items, then V must have the same value at the end of the subroutine. If V is changed, then it could cause another subroutine to be selected, unwanted, when the first subroutine returned, or it could cause the program to hang up with an error message.

The subroutines

The separate actions of the menu have to be carried out by the subroutines. As I have hinted, each subroutine should be designed like a separate program by itself. A complex program might require that each subroutine had its own menu, in which case you will have to go through the actions of menu design for each one. Whether this is needed or not, your aim must always be to break down the action into steps that can be tackled in order, always leaving details to the end.

Suppose, for example, that we have assessed the ENTER ITEMS menu choice as being the most important one whose subroutine must be attended to first. You start the design of this subroutine by deciding what items are to be entered (number, string?), how you expect the screen to look as each item is entered (any prompts?), and how entry is to be terminated (enter $\emptyset$, "X" ?). The next step is to decide how we detect errors (at entry, on a review later?), what mugtraps to use, whether a review of all the entries is needed. We may decide, for example, that we want a simple numbered list for entry, using an INPUT instruction, and that we want to test each entry for an obvious error and then list all entries later as a further check. There is no need at this point to become bogged down in details of how to test and review items – simply write these sections as separate subroutine calls. Figure 5.5 shows how this would be done in our example. The first three lines are taken up with a title and brief instructions. Note that we need some method of terminating entry. When a fixed number of items is to be entered, we can control the entry with a FOR ... NEXT loop so that entry will cease automatically when the correct number of items has been entered. In this case, we might want to print a warning on the screen such as "THIS IS THE LAST ITEM" just to remind the user. Yes, it's another subroutine – we can plan it later. In other cases, we might program for an entered limit, meaning that at an early stage in the

```
10 GOSUB1500
20 END
1000 PRINTTAB(20-LEN(TT$)/2)TT$:RETURN
1500 PRINT"⬛":TT$="ENTRY OF ITEMS":GOSUB1000
1510 PRINT"PLEASE TYPE ITEM WHEN PROMPTED BY ?"
1520 PRINT"TYPE 0 AS AN ITEM TO END ENTRY."
1530 N=1
1540 PRINTN;:INPUT A$
1550 GOSUB10000:REM CHECK INPUT
1560 N=N+1:GOSUB10300
1570 IF A$="0" THEN 1580
1575 A$(N)=A$:GOTO1540
1580 PRINT" DO YOU WANT TO REVIEW?":PRINT"
(ANSWER Y OR N)"
1590 GOSUB10100:REM Y/N REPLY
1600 IF AN$="Y"THEN GOSUB 10200:REM REVIEW
SUBROUTINE.
1610 RETURN:REM TO CALLING ROUTINE
10000 REM CHECK
10010 RETURN
10100 GET AN$:IF AN$=""THEN10100
10110 IF AN$="Y"OR AN$="N"THEN RETURN
10120 PRINT"YOUR REPLY ";AN$" IS NOT UNDERSTOOD."
10130 PRINT"PLEASE TRY AGAIN - Y OR N."
10140 GOTO10100
10200 PRINT"REVIEW NOW....."
10210 RETURN
10300 IF N>10 THEN PRINT"END OF ENTRY":A$="0"
10310 IF N=10 THEN PRINT"LAST ITEM"
10320 RETURN
```

Fig. 5.5. A typical data entry subroutine. The checking that can be carried out depends on the type of data that you want to use.

```
10 GOSUB1500
20 END
1000 PRINTTAB(20-LEN(TT$)/2)TT$:RETURN
1500 PRINT"⬛":TT$="ENTRY OF ITEMS":GOSUB1000
1510 INPUT"HOW MANY ITEMS";NR
1520 DIM A$(NR):FORCOUNT=1TONR
1530 PRINTCOUNT;:INPUT A$(CO)
1540 NEXT
1550 RETURN
```

Fig. 5.6. Checking for the number of entries, so that an array can be correctly dimensioned.

subroutine, the user would be asked:

HOW MANY ENTRIES WILL YOU USE?

This suggestion is dealt with in Fig. 5.6. The only snag with this system is that an incorrect entry of this number, perhaps because you miscounted or because another item turns up that was overlooked, can cause problems. It can also be difficult to add an item once the list has been prepared. The advantage of the system, as with the fixed-number entry system, is that the array of inputs, shown as A$ in the example, can be dimensioned very precisely. This dimensioning can be done in a line immediately following the input of the number of items, so that we could add:

1515 DIM A$(NR)

to carry this out.

When 'free-entry' is used, with no obvious preset limit, we are still restricted, when we use an array, by the dimensioning of the array. If the value of N in the example of Fig. 5.5 becomes greater than the value dimensioned in the core part of the program (which is not illustrated here), then the program will halt with an error message. To avoid this, we shall need a subroutine (see Fig. 5.5) which tests N to check that it is not about to exceed the dimensioned limit.

Note, however, the important points. If we put the details into subroutines, then these subroutines can be written later as we become clearer about what we need. These subroutines might call others in turn, and if we are careful about our variable names we should be able to make use of these same subroutines at other parts of the program. When, for example, we come to the UPDATE PREVIOUS LIST part of the program, it's highly likely that all of the subroutines that we have used in the ENTER ITEMS choice will again be useful. Some subroutines may be useful during review and correction of items, some in the selection of items from the list, and so on. Any piece of program that solves a problem which can turn up elsewhere is a good candidate for a subroutine. Any piece of program which needs more thought or more information before you can write the lines of BASIC is also a candidate for a subroutine. Only when the planning is complete do you start to write these final subroutines.

Some useful routines

When you program in this top-down way, you will often find that you use the same subroutines over and over again in your programs. If you can keep a set of these subroutines on tape or on disk, in addition to your core programs, perhaps, then the physical effort of typing is greatly reduced. Some of the subroutines that you will use are so often employed that they will appear in virtually every program that you write. Of these, the most common 'universal' routines are these concerned with the reading and writing of data on tape or disk.

The 64, following the methods that were established by its ancestors, allows data to be 'connected' to various devices by specifying a code number, $\emptyset$ for the screen, 1 for the cassette system, 4 for the printer, and 8 for the disk system. The ability to transfer data out of the computer is something that the computer has to organise, so that instructions are needed to assist it in this task. The first of these organisation instructions is to 'open a file', meaning that the data is arranged with a filename by which it can be identified. On the 64, as on a number of other computers, this is done by means of the OPEN instruction, which is followed by at least two numbers. Of these numbers, the first is a reference number which the computer uses as a means of recognising the group of data. The numbers used here can be in the range $\emptyset$ to 255, and obvious choices are numbers like 1,2,3, ... etc. The second number is the device number chosen from the list of $\emptyset$,1, 4, and 8 as noted above. The third number, if used, is called the 'secondary address' and is used for supplementary information, such as whether a cassette file is to be written or read, or how the printer is to be controlled.

Suppose, for example, that we want to 'open a file' to send data to the cassette recorder. If we pick reference number 1, then the statement that we need will be:

OPEN 1,1,2

which selects reference number 1, selects the cassette recorder, and selects a write operation with an end-of-tape marker. The OPEN instruction, however, does not cause any of the data to be recorded on the tape. When the OPEN instruction is carried out, the message PRESS RECORD AND PLAY ON TAPE will appear, and when you follow this instruction, the screen will clear and the tape will start as usual. What is being recorded is a 'leader', consisting of recognition signals that the computer will use to identify this data file when the tape is replayed. To carry out the data recording action, we now need to use the instruction PRINT#, along with the same reference number, and specifying the data variable names that we want to record. If we use PRINT#1,A$, for example, we shall record A$ with reference number 1, which is the one allocated to the cassette recorder. If we want to record a set of items whose number is contained in the number variable NR, and which consist of an array A$, then we can use:

```
FOR J = 1 TO NR
PRINT#1,A$(J)
NEXT
```

which will gather the set of items and record them on the tape. Since we normally choose to write the items with an end-of-file marker, we can read the items in until the end of file mark is received, or we can precede the recording of the data with a recording of the maximum number of items, NR in this example, using:

```
PRINT#1,NR
```

It's up to you to choose – the method of recording NR separately is probably easier for many purposes until you are familiar with data filing methods and since the manual illustrates the use of an end-of-file marker (any item which can be recognised, like the number 999 or the string "END"), we'll show the alternative. Note that an end-of-file marker is not the same as an *end-of-tape* marker. The end-of-tape marker will prevent the machine from reading any more files from the same tape unless the tape is removed and re-inserted.

It is particularly important, after a file has been recorded, to close the file, using the instruction CLOSE 1 (the example is for the cassette file in the illustration). The use of CLOSE records any remaining data on to the tape, so that if this is omitted, only part of the data may be recorded. In addition, the machine will not act correctly if a file is not closed correctly.

Our cassette-filing program subroutine will therefore look as Fig. 5.7 – I have used the line numbers that were used in the menu program of Fig. 5.1. The important features of the program, apart from the use of the OPEN and the PRINT# commands are the messages. As well as the messages that the machine operating system delivers, such as PRESS RECORD AND PLAY ON TAPE, one message announces that data is about to be recorded, another announces that recording is complete. Each message is followed by a "PRESS ANY KEY" step which should really be put into a subroutine because it is invariably used many times in a program of this type. These messages are essential to let the user of the program know what is going on. There is nothing worse than a program

```
10 FORN=1TO5
20 PRINT"ENTER A NAME"
30 INPUT A$(N)
40 NEXT
50 NR=5
60 GOSUB2000
70 END
2000 OPEN1,1,2
2010 PRINT"DATA WILL NOW BE RECORDED"
2020 PRINT"PLEASE PREPARE RECORDER.":PRINT"PRESS
ANY KEY WHEN READY"
2030 GET K$:IF K$=""THEN2030
2040 PRINT#1,NR
2050 FORJ=1TONR
2060 PRINT#1,A$(J)
2070 NEXT:CLOSE1
2080 PRINT"◻":PRINT"END OF RECORDING"
2090 PRINT"PRESS ANY KEY TO PROCEED"
2100 GET K$:IF K$=""THEN2100
2110 RETURN
```

Fig. 5.7. A subroutine for data filing on cassette.

```
2∅ OPEN 1,∅ : REM SCREEN IS 1
25 OPEN 2,1,1 :REM CASSETTE WRITE 2
3∅ OPEN 3,4 :REM PRINTER IS 3
35 OPEN 4,1,∅ :REM CASSETTE READ 4
......................................................................
......................................................................
5∅∅∅ N = 1 :REM SELECT SCREEN
5∅1∅ PRINT#N,"DATA":IF N=3 THEN 5∅3∅
5∅2∅ N=3:GOTO 5∅1∅
5∅3∅ GOSUB 6∅∅∅ :REM CASSETTE MESSAGE
5∅4∅ N=2 :REM CASSETTE WRITE
5∅5∅ FOR J = 1 TO NR
5∅6∅ PRINT#N, A$(J)
5∅7∅ NEXT
......................................................................
```

Fig. 5.8. Using the PRINT # instruction to direct data to various destinations or to receive data from various sources.

which gives the user no indication of what he/she is supposed to do next. Even if you write and use the program yourself, you may easily forget what the intention was – when the screen stops changing do you start the recorder, press any key, or just wait? Messages avoid these problems.

The PRINT# command is a general type of instruction which means 'put the data out on a line with a stated reference number'. The line 1, as we have set it up in the example, causes cassette recording. If we make every PRINT in the program into a PRINT#N, then by using different values of N, we can direct data to the cassette recorder, to the screen, to the printer or to a disk system. The general method is illustrated in Fig. 5.8 – though this has not been tested, since I did not have a printer or a working disk system. A set of OPEN instructions early in the program allocates the reference numbers, and wherever we would use a PRINT instruction, we place PRINT N in its place. In this way, by allocating N, we can choose whether to place the data on the screen, to the printer, to tape, or to the disk system. It's important to note, however, that you must not attempt to send data to or read data from devices which are not connected. This can cause the computer to hang up, and it is not always possible to recover your program when this happens.

The most common switch of destination of data is between the screen and the printer, so that the 64 uses a special instruction, CMD for this purpose. If, for example, the printer is on line number 3, then the instruction CMD3 will send all PRINT items to the printer in place of the screen. The snag is that to reverse the instruction you have to close the line, using CLOSE 3. Having done

```
10 GOSUB2500
20 END
2500 PRINT"⊃":PRINT"PLEASE PREPARE TO READ DATA"
2510 PRINT"PREPARE RECORDER-PRESS ANY KEY TO
START"
2520 GET K$:IF K$=""THEN2520
2530 OPEN5,1,0:REM READ
2540 INPUT#5,NR
2560 FORJ=1TONR
2570 INPUT#5,A$(J):NEXT
2580 CLOSE5
2590 FORJ=1TONR:PRINT A$(J):NEXT
2600 RETURN
```

Fig. 5.9. A data-file reading subroutine.

this, a new OPEN 3,4 will have to be used if the printer is to be used again.

Reading files from cassette or disk requires the use of OPEN along with INPUT#, followed by the reference number that has been used in the OPEN instruction. As for writing, the file should be closed when the reading is complete. This does not mean when one item, or even a list of items, has been read, but only when all file reading has been completed – omitting CLOSE in a reading program will not cause the loss of data as it might in a tape-writing program. A good place to put the CLOSE instruction is at the end of the subroutine that deals with reading.

Figure 5.9 shows a typical file reading subroutine which uses reference number 5 for the input file. This program will read the data that was recorded by the writing program of Fig. 5.7.

Other subroutines

In the course of a data processing program, certain subroutines tend to be used more than others, and some subroutines appear in practically every program that you use. In general, you will gather a collection of subroutines as your experience of writing such programs grows, and there are books available, such as my own *Some Useful Basic Subroutines* (Newnes) which list, with comments, subroutines that are particularly useful. Of the longer subroutines, the most useful are these which deal with string arrays. A string-search subroutine, for example, will hunt through a string array looking for a string with specified characteristics. These may be initial letter, groups of letters, length of string or other distinguishing features. An alphabetical sort is another subroutine which is likely to feature in most data processing programs. Most books illustrate sorting programs with reference to a type known as the bubble-sort, which has the distinction of being the least efficient of all sorting methods, and one which should be avoided at all costs if several hundred items are to be sorted. The time difference between a bubble-sort and a more efficient type, such as the Shell-Metzner sort, can be several hours!

Chapter Six
Introducing Graphics

Graphics characters are shapes that can be used to create pictures rather than text (numbers or letters) on the screen of the TV or monitor. Graphics characters have obvious uses in games and other leisure-programs, but they also have applications to business programs. The display of bar charts, for example, can be very useful in such programs, as can drawing of graphs and other aids to the comprehension of figures. Pictorial aids may also be surprisingly useful to help concentrate attention on important information.

The standard graphics characters of the 64 are the symbols that appear on the keys, and which can be entered into programs directly just like any other characters that are printed on the keys. It is possible, for example, to mix graphics with text so as to create underlinings and borders, as Fig. 6.1 shows. One program listing (Fig.

```
10 TT$="●●●●●●●● TITLE ●●●●●●●●":PRINT"⏌"
20 GOSUB1000:REM PRINT AT CENTRE
30 TT$="++++++++++++++++++++++++++":GOSUB1000
40 END
1000 PRINTTAB(20-LEN(TT$)/2)TT$:RETURN
```
(a)

```
10 TT$="[8G>Q] [SPC] TITLE[SPC] [8G<Q]"
20 GOSUB 1000:REM PRINT AT CENTRE
30 TT$="[23G>+8G>Q]":GOSUB 1000
40 END
1000 PRINTTAB (20-LEN(TT$)/2)TT$:RETURN
```

(b)

Fig. 6.1. Using keyboard graphics. (a) Printed version, showing the appearance of the listing on the screen. (b) Typed version using C.T. standards.

6.1(a)) has been produced from a printer in this case and the other (Fig. 6.1(b)) has been written using the C.T. standards for indicating special key functions. These standards were pioneered by the magazine, *Computing Today*, to whom I am grateful for permission to reproduce the items shown in Fig. 6.2. The square brackets indicate

---

1. Use of SHIFT key.

[ ]	square brackets indicate use of graphics keys
5	number indicates number of times used
∧	symbol for shift key
H	followed by normal letter shown on key
[5 ∧ H]	Example – press SHIFT H 5 times

2. Use symbols to right or left of keys, and special keys.

[CLS]	Clear the screen
[HOM]	Home the cursor
[CL]	Move cursor left
[CR]	Move cursor right
[CU]	Move cursor up
[CD]	Move cursor down
[REV]	Reverse video on
[OFF]	Turn effect off
[SPC]	Space
[CTL]	Control key
[fn]	Programmable function key
[G<]	Graphic symbol on left hand side
[G>]	Graphic symbol on right hand side

Fig. 6.2. The C.T. standards for typing listings that contain non-printable characters.

the use of keys for other than alphabetical or numeric/punctuation characters. The symbol, [G<], for example, means the graphics-left, which is the graphics symbol on the left-hand side of the key. [G>] would similarly mean the graphics symbol on the right hand side of the key. On the 64, the graphics-right symbols are obtained by pressing the SHIFT key along with the character key when the machine is working in program mode (*not* in upper-case/lower-case mode). The graphics left symbols are obtained by pressing the Commodore key (⌨) and the SHIFT key together, followed by the Commodore key (⌨) along with the character key.

In Fig. 6.1 the string starts with [8G>Q], meaning press SHIFT Q (to get the right hand side graphics on the Q key) eight times. This is followed by a space [SPC], then the word TITLE, and the same border pattern is then repeated in reverse order. This string is printed centred by the subroutine at line 1∅∅∅, and then the string is redefined as 23 presses of the graphics symbol on the right hand side of the + key, which is the chequerboard pattern. This is also printed centred by the subroutine.

The effect of the graphics addition is to highlight the title, and the effect will be enhanced if colour is used (see Chapter Seven). There is a wide choice of characters that can be used for these purposes, though some of them are obviously designed to be used with games programs rather than for business applications. If you are mixing graphics characters with text it makes sense to try to use the right hand graphics as far as possible, because these need only the use of the SHIFT key when the machine is in program mode. If you use lower-case text, you will have to become used to the procedure for shifting back to program mode for graphics entry.

Field marking

One notable use for graphics characters in data processing is to provide more visual information when the INPUT instruction is used. Data processing programs often require the entry of data in a set format, and graphics characters can be used to ensure that this is

```
10 PRINT"⌂":TT$="xxx INPUT xxx"
20 GOSUB1000:PRINT:PRINT:LT$="":NR$=""
30 PRINT"    |||     000";
40 PRINT"■■■■■■■■■■■";
50 FORN=1TO4:GOSUB500:PRINT A$;
60 LT$=LT$+A$:NEXT
70 PRINT"     ";
80 FOR N=1TO3:GOSUB500:PRINT A$;
90 NR$=NR$+A$:NEXT
100 PRINT:PRINT
110 PRINT"REFERENCE IS ";LT$+NR$
120 END
500 GET A$:IF A$=""THEN500
505 REM TEST FOR VALUE HERE
510 RETURN
1000 PRINTTAB(20-LEN(TT$)/2)TT$:RETURN
```

Fig. 6.3. Using a 'fielded' input. This is very commonly used in data processing programs.

correctly done. Suppose, for example, that we have to enter codes that consist of four letters and three digits. When this is done using the normal input methods, a reminder must be printed, and even this cannot prevent mistakes. A 'fielded' input can help here by reducing the possibility of error. This uses graphics characters to indicate the numbers of each type of character to be entered, and the characters that are typed in will replace the graphics characters so that the operator can see at a glance how the entry is progressing and if anything is left undone. An example of this type of programming is illustrated in Fig. 6.3, in which a four-letter and three-digit entry is called for and GET is used in place of input. GET is used within a subroutine so that if an incorrect entry is made it will be possible to correct this either during entry or at a subsequent review. A conventional INPUT can be used to allow more time for second thoughts – some programmers prefer this to the use of GET because it allows time to check the entry after the last character has been typed.

Graphics strings

As we saw in Fig. 6.1 a set of graphics characters can be printed by treating the characters as if they were ordinary keyboard characters. We can also incorporate these characters into strings as we did in Fig. 6.3, with or without other text.

The advantage of incorporating graphics characters into strings is that the whole string can be printed at different parts of the screen. We can position the printing by using the TAB across the screen and the down-arrow character to move down the screen. It is possible to make up a string that contains, both graphics characters and cursor-shift characters (up, down, left, right), so that a pattern will appear on the screen when the string is printed. This can, for example, be used to considerable effect as a company logo, or for any other distinguishing mark. The Commodore printer will reproduce all of the 64 graphics characters, so that the creation of a company logo shape which can also be printed on paper is fairly easy. Some other printers, notably the Epson series, permit any graphics pattern to be reproduced by sending control codes and numbers to the printer, but this is by no means so straightforward as the use of the Commodore printer.

Figure 6.4 shows a typical logo created by using graphics characters, and printed at the centre of the screen, on which text can also be printed. A subroutine for clearing the text part of the screen, but leaving the logo undisturbed is also included. The printing of the

```
10 LG$=" ⌒  ⌒▒▒▒▒▒▒▒▌◡  ◡▒▒▒▒▒▒▌|  |"
15 PRINT"⌐"
20 PRINTTAB(19)LG$
```

Fig. 6.4. A simple 'logo' created from graphics characters.

symbol is greatly simplified by the fact that the logo can be printed by the simple command PRINT LG$, rather than by the laborious method of printing each character separately. This is a considerable advantage for the use of keyboard graphics – there are several machines which claim advanced graphics capability, but which cannot make use of this method.

Another advantage of containing a complete pattern of graphics characters in the form of a string is that animation is possible. Animation is achieved by printing the string at some position on the screen, then after a short time interval, deleting this string, and printing the pattern, slightly displaced. If this process of print, delete, print displaced is carried out in succession over several print positions, the pattern will appear to move across the screen, up or down, according to the direction of shifting. More complex movements can be carried out by using a combination of these movements. Figure 6.5 shows an illustration of a simple pattern which is moved into place and then used as the 'frame' for a title.

```
10 TT$="O¬O"
20 PRINT"⌐":FORN=0TO19
30 PRINTTAB(N)TT$;:PRINT"▒▒▒▌";
40 FORJ=1TO50:NEXT
50 PRINT"    ";:PRINT"▒▒▒▌";
60 NEXT
70 PRINTTAB(19)TT$
```

Fig. 6.5. Animating a graphics string so as to create a moving logo.

POKE graphics

Graphics characters and strings can be put into place by the PRINT instruction, but there is also a faster system which makes use of the keyword POKE. POKE means 'put into memory', and has to be followed by a position number, called an 'address', and a data number. The address number decides where the data number is to be stored, so that the instruction POKE 1Ø24,48 will place the number code 48 into memory location 1024. POKE is an instruction that has to be used with some discrimination, because any part of the usable memory can be affected by it. If you POKE a number into the wrong address it may have the effect of sabotaging the operating system of the computer. This won't cause any physical damage, but it may cause the computer to go into what looks like a trance, with nothing new appearing on the screen, and no response to the keyboard. To get out of this state, tap the RUN/STOP and RESTORE keys. The worst that can happen to you when you get a 'system crash' like this is that you lose the program that you were working on. The moral is always to record a program before you try it – this applies to modified versions of programs for which you already have a recording. Personally, I keep a cassette just for developing each program so that I have a version of each stage in development.

The screen of the 64 is 'memory mapped', which means that each printable position on the screen has a memory address dedicated to it. Printing a character on the screen corresponds to placing the number code for that character into the corresponding memory address, so that the POKE instruction can be used to carry out PRINT actions. The difference is that the POKE action can be used for any point on the screen, selected at random, whereas the PRINT action is carried out in sequence, left to right in each line, and moving down from one line to the next. The other difference is that POKE deals with one code, one character, at a time, whereas PRINT can be used to place a whole string of characters onto the screen. The PRINT instruction, in fact, is a form of POKE to the screen addresses used with a loop.

Figure 6.6 shows an example of POKE at work. The screen memory uses 1000 addresses. This is because the screen permits 25

```
10 PRINT"⊐":POKE53281,3:FORN=1024TO1984STEP40
20 READ J$:POKEN,ASC(J$)-64:NEXT
30 DATAS,C,R,E,E,N,X,P,O,K,E,X,D,E,M,O,N,S,T,R,
A,T,I,O,N
```

Fig. 6.6. Using the POKE instruction. Note the instruction which changes the colour so that the poked characters are visible.

lines of 40 characters per line, which means that a total of 1000 character positions are used. The memory addresses are 1024 to 2023 inclusive, and a POKE to any of these positions will affect the screen picture. This screen layout is illustrated in Fig. 6.7. The address numbers refer to the positions for the start of each line, with the tabulation numbers 0 to 39 added to the start-of-line address number

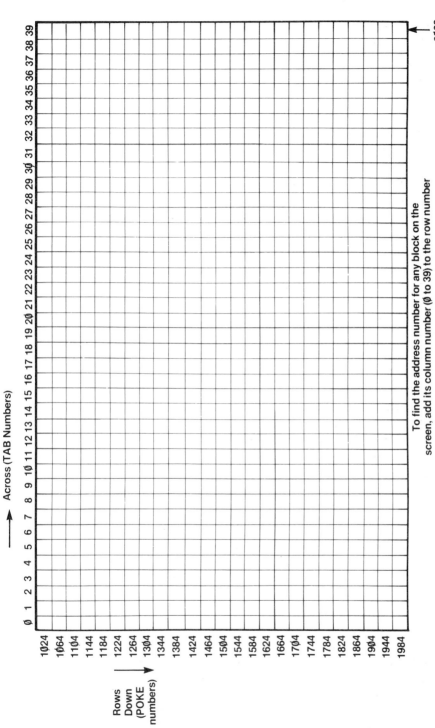

Fig. 6.7. The screen 'memory map' layout.

to find the position of any point in a line. The starting address, 1Ø24 is the HOME position of the cursor, the top left-hand corner; the finishing point of 2Ø23 is at the bottom right-hand corner of the screen. A minor complication is that a code POKEd to these addresses produces no visible effect until either the colour of the character or of the background is changed. In Fig. 6.6 the background colour has been changed.

If we place character code numbers in the first memory address of each line, the effect will be to print a column on the screen, and this is what the program of Fig. 6.6 does. The FOR ... NEXT loop starts with the first memory address, the HOME address, and goes in steps of 40 so that it progresses from 1Ø24 to 1Ø64, 11Ø4, 1144, and so on, which are the first character positions of each line. Into each of these addresses, the program pokes an ASCII code number, and by using ASC(J$), we select the ASCII code number of the letter which has been read by the READ ... DATA instruction. The effect is therefore to place the words into column form at the left hand side of the screen.

The very considerable advantage of using the POKE instruction is that it does not affect the cursor position. We can use POKE to place individual characters anywhere on the screen, and then return to print instructions which will be placed at the cursor position. In games programs, this can be used for the rapid printing of patterns or for moving single characters around. For data processing programs, the POKE facility offers a way of drawing bar charts, graphs, and other diagrams.

Suppose, for example, that we want to chart the pre-tax profits of a small business over a period of four years. We shall need to know the starting year and the figure of pre-tax profits each year, so that we can use these figures to construct the chart. We'll imagine for the sake of simplicity that the maximum profit level is £200,000 and that we shall represent this on the chart by a bar which is 20 lines high.

The program example is shown in Fig. 6.8. Lines 1Ø to 5Ø obtain the range of years and the profit figure for each year. The profit figure must be between £1Ø,ØØØ and £2ØØ,ØØØ for this particular program – imposing these limits allows us to keep the program simple and to demonstrate bar chart drawing without the excessive complications of being able to adjust the scales to fit any range of data that was used.

Line 7Ø contains a time delay, simply to give you time between entering the last value and seeing the bars appear. The title is then printed, and line 9Ø calculates how many steps of £1Ø,ØØØ units are needed to represent each amount. INT is used because we will use a graphics block to represent £1Ø,ØØØ amounts, and we cannot so easily

```
10 PRINT"⬛":TT$="PROFITS":GOSUB1000
20 PRINT:INPUT"STARTING YEAR";SY
30 FOR YR=SY TO SY+3
40 PRINT"PROFIT FOR YEAR ";YR;" IS ";
50 GOSUB 1200
60 NEXT:PRINT"PLEASE WAIT"
70 FOR N=1 TO 1000:NEXT
80 TT$="PROFITS CHART":GOSUB 1000
90 FOR N=1 TO 4:BH(N)=INT(PR(N)/10000)
95 PRINTTAB(5*N-1)N;
100 NEXT:BA=1904
105 POKE53281,3
110 FOR N=1TO4
120 FOR J=1 TO BH(N)
130 POKE BA+5*N-40*J,102
140 NEXT
150 NEXT
160 GET A$:IF A$=""THEN 160
200 END
1000 PRINT"⬛":PRINTTAB(20-LEN(TT$)/2)TT$:RETURN
1200 INPUT P
1210 IF P>200000 THEN PRINT"TOO LARGE":GOTO1240
1220 IF P<10000 THEN PRINT "TOO SMALL":GOTO 1240
1230 PR(YR-SY+1)=P:RETURN
1240 PRINT"AGAIN, PLEASE";:GOTO1200
```

Fig. 6.8. A simple bar chart program to illustrate the use of POKE instructions.

use half-blocks without introducing considerable complications into the program. The variable BH for each profit figure will therefore be the number of complete blocks for each bar.

Line 100 finishes the loop and sets the final address in the bottom line of the screen as the variable BA. The bars are then drawn in the loops starting in lines 110 and 120. The FOR N = 1 TO 4 loop ensures that a bar will be drawn for each of the profit figures. The next loop, FOR J = 1 TO BH(N) will decide how high to draw each bar, because BH(N) is the number of graphics blocks in each bar. The POKE instructions in line 130 then puts each graphics block into place. By using the formula that is shown, for one value of N, the graphics block will always be placed on the same position along each line, but by using 40 * J, one block is placed on top of another for as many times as the value of BH determines. When a pile of graphics blocks has been stacked up for a bar, the J-loop ends, and the next N loop begins, tracing the next bar in the same way. The year numbers have previously (in line 95) been printed at the top of the screen. The program finally enters a loop in line 16∅ to prevent the cursor from appearing. Obviously, this bar chart program could be written as a subroutine so that it could be used within another program. If it is impossible to place into the program in advance the maximum range of the quantities that will be charted, then an autoscaling subroutine must be used. A suitable routine is illustrated in Fig. 6.9. In this example, the size of each

```
10 Z=10:FOR J=1TOZ
20 N(J)=RND(1)*99+1
30 NEXT
40 GOSUB5000
50 FORJ=1TOZ:PRINT N(J):NEXT
60 PRINT"MAXIMUM IS ";MX
70 END
5000 MX=N(1):FOR J=1 TO Z
5010 IF MX<N(J)THEN MX=N(J)
5020 NEXT:RETURN
```

Fig. 6.9. A routine for finding the maximum value in a set of numbers. This can then be used to scale the barchart, making the maximum value apply to, say, 20 blocks and using proportional values for other numbers.

entry is checked, and the maximum size of entry is used to represent the maximum height of bar that will be plotted.

A bar chart program is much easier to produce if the bars are horizontal rather than vertical, because when the number of blocks is known, a string can be packed with the required number and then printed. The vertical bar diagram is more common, however, and has been used so as to illustrate POKE graphics in a business application. If you want a mental exercise, try modifying the program so that the bars are much wider – perhaps five character widths per bar.

Using PEEK

The keyword PEEK performs the opposite of POKE by providing the number that is stored at a given memory address. The syntax is PEEK(address), and the PEEK must be used in a PRINT statement (PRINT PEEK(1∅24)); as an assignment (P%=PEEK(1∅24)) or as a test (IF PEEK(1∅24) = 32 THEN ...). The value of PEEK in a graphics program is that it can be used to test what is stored in the memory and in particular on the screen. PEEK can be used, for example, to find if a memory location is occupied, and to cause an appropriate reaction.

Try the program in Fig. 6.10. This reproduces a phrase on the screen – but inverts the pattern of the printed line! The value SR (for

```
10 PRINT"⏏";:K=439:SR=1024
20 PRINT"THIS IS A TEST"
30 FORN=39 TO 0 STEP-1
40 POKESR+K-N,PEEK(SR+N)
45 POKE53281,15
50 NEXT
```

Fig. 6.10. Using POKE to create a pattern inversion.

START) is the address of the first position of the top line on the screen, and the constant K has been chosen as 439, an interval of almost eleven lines. In the loop that starts at line 30, the values of N run from 39 to 0, so that in the first run the POKE SR+K−N gives an address number of 1024 + 439 − 39, which is 1424, the address of the start of the tenth line. The PEEK, however, is from SR + N, which is 1063, the end of the first line. On the next run through the loop, the value of N is 38, so that the POKE is to 1425, the second position of the tenth line, and the PEEK is from 1062, one space from the right hand side of the first line. In this way, the characters are read from the first line in inverse order and printed in the tenth line in this order starting at the left hand side. It may look pointless when carried out on text in this way, but it's a useful way of printing symmetrical patterns when you use graphics blocks in place of letters.

We can also use PEEK in useful processing operations, such as replacing dollar signs by pound signs (for use by printers), or in converting one graphics character into another. Suppose, for example, that we wish to reproduce a pattern on the screen using a printer which is not able to reproduce Commodore graphics directly. By testing each screen location, using a loop such as:

FOR N% = 1024 TO 2023
K% = PEEK(N%)

then each character code is assigned to the variable K%, and we can test:

IF K%>127 THEN GOSUB 5000

This test will detect the use of a graphics code (with numbers greater than 63), and call a subroutine which will substitute some other code or a set of codes to send to the printer. Line 5∅∅∅ will contain the instruction:

K$ = GR$(K%)

with GR$ being the set of codes corresponding to the number K%. We would need to have defined these codes, and the complete string of codes would then have to be converted into numbers to send to the printer. This is particularly applicable to printers such as the Epson Mk.3 which has definable graphics, meaning that it will print a pattern defined by a set of number codes sent to it. Note the use of integer variables in the program, since each address number and the number stored in it must be an integer.

Planning block graphics

Another use for graphics in data processing programs is the provision of large title letters and emblems. These can be put into the form of strings, as we noted earlier in this chapter, or they can be poked piece by piece into the screen memory directly. Either way, some planning is needed.

Planning graphics is most easily done if a good screen-plan diagram is available. Figure 6.7 showed a screen diagram which indicated character positions, along with both the POKE numbers and the TAB numbers. By laying tracing paper over this grid and using a pencil, you can design your pattern by shading in blocks on the screen to show the appearance of the graphics pattern that you want. Designers tend to work in negative, meaning that a shaded block will, in fact, appear on the screen as white or in other foreground colours, rather than in black as the paper drawing suggests. Until we have black paper and white pencils, this will have to be the way we do it, but if you want to work in 'real' shades, there is no reason why you should not, except that it usually involves more work.

Creating simple geometrical patterns can often be most simply dealt with by using POKE instructions, but other patterns are most easily dealt with by assigning the characters to strings and then printing them with the appropriate TAB numbers. Unlike the 'pixel' graphics shapes that are used in other computers, the graphics shapes of the 64 have been designed with some thought to their combination into patterns. The graphics shapes on keys U,I,J, and K, for example, are sections of a circle which can be combined to create a circular shape that occupies the intersections of four character blocks. The four basic playing-card patterns of spades, hearts, diamonds and clubs are on keys A,S,Z, and X, and the patterns of diagonals on keys N and M are useful as cross-hatching.

Video inversion

In addition to the patterns that are shown on the keys, the inverse patterns, in which foreground and background colours are swapped, can be obtained. The keys which carry the 9 and ∅ symbols on top also have the words R VS ON and R VS OFF (respectively) printed on their sloping fronts. When the Commodore key (C=) is pressed at the same time as the '9' key, the effect is to start reverse video, so that everything typed from then on has the foreground and the background colours reversed. If, for example you were typing in white on black, then pressing CTL 9 to put R VS ON would then cause typing to be black on white. Being able to reverse the video like this has the effect of adding another set of graphics characters, because everything that can be placed on the screen in normal video can also be used in inverse video. The reverse video can be switched off by using CTL ∅, RVS OFF. As usual, the codes for these actions can be typed into strings, as Fig. 6.11 shows.

```
10 PRINT"THIS IS IN NORMAL VIDEO"
20 PRINT" THIS IS IN INVERSE VIDEO"
30 PRINT"  O  ♠"
```

Fig. 6.11. Using reverse video codes within strings.

Chapter Seven
Sprites and Colour

The graphics patterns that are obtainable from the keyboard are preformed patterns which are classed as low-resolution, meaning that only 4∅ × 25 character positions can be used. The 64 also has the capability to create graphics characters to your own design. These are high resolution, meaning that they make use of the screen as if it consisted of 32∅ dots across by 2∅∅ dots deep, with each dot individually controllable. In addition, these graphics patterns can be moved about the screen and it is possible to assign priorities to them so that one pattern will always appear to pass 'in front' of another when two patterns cross. These movable graphics patterns are known as 'sprites' or, less imaginatively, as MOBS (Mobile Object BlockS).

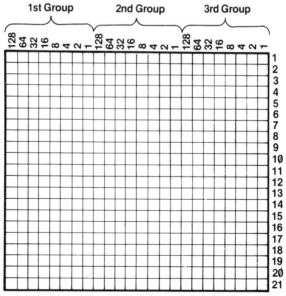

Fig. 7.1. Sprite planning grid. Don't attempt to use fine detail, because the sprite is a very small block on the screen. For large objects, you can magnify the display, or use more than one sprite.

The use of sprite graphics involves considerably more work than the use of the keyboard graphics, but it enables you to create any patterns that you wish, subject to the size and complexity of the pattern, and to move these patterns with considerable freedom. Sprites are planned on a grid, illustrated in Fig. 7.1, which is made up of 24 units across by 21 units deep. By placing a piece of tracing paper over this grid and working with a soft pencil, you can create your own pattern whose actual size on a 14″ TV receiver, if you have used the full grid, is about 15 mm by 10 mm.

These sprite patterns are controlled by a separate set of controls within the 64. These controls allow you to create up to eight sprites at any time on the screen, to move them independently, detect collisions, and change their colours. As you might expect, all of this requires a considerable amount of programming effort.

The method by which you, the programmer, create and control sprites is by the use of address numbers in the memory. The keyword to changing the contents of these memory addresses is the POKE instruction which we used earlier to control normal screen graphics Sprites are created and controlled by using POKE instructions to the special memory addresses that are reserved for the sprites. The numbers that are used for the POKE instructions are normal denary numbers (decimal numbers), but these represent the values of binary numbers. The binary (scale of two) numbers represent the positions of 1's and ∅'s in sets of eight, one set of eight to a memory address, and each 1 or ∅ acts as a signal to the computer. It is these signals which correspond to the details of the sprite patterns, and which are used to select which sprite is moved. Before we can go much further in sprite graphics, then, we have to understand something of binary numbers.

Binary numbers

We write numbers normally by using a scale of ten. This means that we use ten digits, 0 to 9, and that the number ten is indicated by taking a separate column, so that 17 means one ten and seven units, 48 means four tens and eight units, and so on. The next column position is 10×10, equal to 100, so that 285 means two hundreds, eight tens and five units.

Our choice of ten as a 'base', meaning the number at which we take a new column for writing digits, is quite arbitrary, and probably derives from having ten digits on our two hands. Computers, however, use a binary scale, a scale of two, because they count using miniature switches. A switch is either on or off, two possible states, so that the natural counting scale is one that uses the two digits ∅ (for off) and 1 (for on). A count-up in binary would therefore start conventionally with ∅ and then 1, but the next number will be two, meaning one 'two' and zero units. This is written as 1∅, using the position to the left of the zero (units column) to indicate the number of twos (the twos column). The next number in the count is 11 (a two and a unit, equal to three), and for four we have to move another place over to the left, writing the number as 1∅∅.

Denary	Binary
∅	∅∅∅∅
1	∅∅∅1
2	∅∅1∅
3	∅∅11
4	∅1∅∅
5	∅1∅1
6	∅11∅
7	∅111
8	1∅∅∅
9	1∅∅1
1∅	1∅1∅
11	1∅11
12	11∅∅
13	11∅1
14	111∅
15	1111

most significant bit ▢▢▢▢ least significant bit

(columns labelled: *eights*, *fours*, *twos*, *units*)

Fig. 7.2. A binary number count.

Figure 7.2 shows a count from ∅ to fifteen, comparing denary numbers with binary numbers so that you can see the sequences of binary digits. Converting a binary number into denary is simple, making use of Fig. 7.3 Each 1 in a binary number occurs at a position which corresponds to some denary value, and this position will be one of these shown in the table. By adding all the denary values corresponding to these '1' positions, the denary value for the binary number is found.

The example shows how the figures are obtained. The relevance of this is that the computer works with 8-digit binary numbers (eight-bit numbers, as they are called), so that each memory address can store a number which, in binary, is between ∅∅∅∅∅∅∅∅ and 11111111. This corresponds in denary to the range ∅ to 255, and it is numbers in

Procedure	*Example*
1. Write binary number (eight bits)	∅ 1 1 ∅ 1 1 1 ∅
2. Write denary value of each 1	64 32 8 4 2
3. Add these values	11∅

Denary Values:

128   64   32   16   8   4   2   1   *Denary numbers*

☐ ☐ ☐ ☐ ☐ ☐ ☐ ☐   *Boxes for binary bits*

Write the binary number into these boxes (use tracing paper), and then note the denary number for each box that contains a 1. Add the denary numbers

Fig. 7.3. Binary – denary conversion.

this range that we can POKE into memory addresses. For graphics purposes, we deal with several blocks of these groups of eight, but the conversion of each block into a denary number is carried out in the same way. The block of eight is called a 'byte', and this is the unit that is used for measuring memory size – 1∅24 bytes is a kilobyte (K).

Practical sprite generation

Let's illustrate the generation of a sprite pattern in the simplest possible way, which is to take an example, and to follow the programming steps in detail. Let's assume that you want to display your mobile-homes emblem, along with the letters CCC (Chislebury Caravan Company), in sprite form. Using a sprite allows you to move the caravan across the screen, and you may later plan a point-of-sale exhibit in which the caravan tows a banner and in which the screen then switches to a sales message. The first act of sprite creation is the planning of the image, so we need to make use of the sprite planning grid. Trace the outline of the sprite lightly, and try to make it as simple as possible unless you are convinced of your artistic abilities. At the moment, it's the main outline of the shape that's important, and Fig. 7.4 shows a suggestion. Take some time over this planning stage – it's by far the most difficult part of sprite production, particularly if you are as inartistic as I am.

The next step is to convert each row of filled-in squares into numbers. The 24-squares across needs three numbers because, as we saw earlier, the computer works with binary numbers that have eight

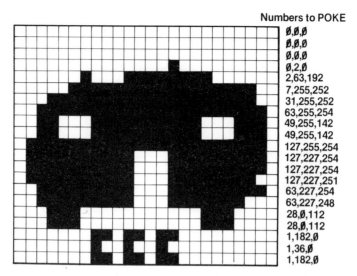

Numbers to POKE

0,0,0
0,0,0
0,0,0
0,2,0
2,63,192
7,255,252
31,255,252
63,255,254
49,255,142
49,255,142
127,255,254
127,227,254
127,227,254
127,227,251
63,227,254
63,227,248
28,0,112
28,0,112
1,182,0
1,36,0
1,182,0

Fig. 7.4. A sprite shape, with the numbers that will be needed to create it.

digits each. Each group of eight binary digits can then be converted into a denary number between 0 and 255 by adding up the denary equivalents. When you have completed the sprite plan, you will have 21 sets of three numbers, 63 numbers in all for each sprite. It's hard work!

Getting back to our pattern, the first three rows of squares are all blank, so that we start with nine zeros (three per row, remember). In row four, there is one shaded square, the ventilator of the caravan, which is in the 2-position of the second group of figures. The numbers for this row will therefore be 0,2,0. In the fifth row, however, we have more to do. The 2-position of the first group is filled, and the 32,16,8,4,2, and 1 positions of the second group are filled. This gives 2 as the first number, and the sum of 32 ..... to 1, which is 63, for the second number. In the third group of this row, the 128 and 64 positions are shaded, making the number 192. The set of three figures for the row is therefore 2,63,192.

We go down the rows in this way, counting the filled squares and writing the groups of numbers. It's useful to remember that a complete set of shaded squares gives the number 255. If the square on the left of the group is missing, the number is 127, and if the square on the right is missing, the number is 254. In other words, if a lot of squares are shaded, it's often easier to subtract than to add numbers. We should now have a set of 21 × 3 = 63 numbers.

These numbers are now typed into DATA lines. You can put them all into one large DATA line (remember the comma between each number and the next) or you can use 21 DATA lines with just three numbers in each. Using 21 DATA lines makes it much easier to change your pattern because there is then a direct relationship between the rows of the pattern and the DATA lines. When you have obtained the final pattern, however, the creation of the sprite will be quicker and will use less memory if you put all the numbers into one long DATA line.

Having completed the DATA for the simple shape, we then have to arrange for the computer to READ these numbers into the correct memory locations and to make use of them. There is one particularly important number involved here – 53248. This is the first number of a set of memory addresses that controls the 'video chip', which is the part of the computer that deals with sprites, so we start any sprite program by allocating this number to a variable. I have chosen the variable name VC to remind me that this is the starting address for the Video Chip. The first useful address for us in the set that starts at VC (equal to 53248) is 21 places on from this starting point, so we can refer to it as VC + 21. This is the address that lets us choose the *level* of the sprite. Level doesn't just mean a reference number for the sprite, it also means relative importance. A level 0 sprite will always appear to pass in front of any other level sprite, for example, so the number indicates priority. This isn't important if you have only one sprite or if you aren't going to move sprites, but it is useful for moving displays where you may want one pattern always to be seen. In our example, the caravan is the only sprite, so we'll give it priority level 7. The priority levels range from 0 to 7 (not 1 to 8 – binary again!) so that this is the lowest priority. This way, if we add other sprites later, the others will always be visible, appearing to pass in front of the caravan when they move around the screen.

The memory at address VC + 21 consists of the usual eight bits, with the usual denary equivalent numbers. The top level is indicated by a 1 in the left-hand position, corresponding to the denary number 128. To establish that this sprite is a level 7 one, then, we need to program:

POKE VC + 21,128

This step will ensure that the sprite has lowest priority, and it also ensures that we can make it appear on the screen when we want it. If we later POKE a 1 into this address, we shall have changed the priority of this sprite to level 0, which is the highest level of priority. A 0 poked into this address will disable the sprite so that it does not appear.

Address	Sprite level
2040	0
2041	1
2042	2
2043	3
2044	4
2045	5
2046	6
2047	7

The number that is POKEd into one of these addresses must be a 'block number'. This indicates which block of memory holds the data numbers for this sprite.

Fig. 7.5. The sprite pointer locations.

The next step is to place the DATA for the sprite shape into the correct memory locations. The memory locations are arranged in blocks of 64, and we need one block for each sprite. This is done in two steps. The first step is to set a 'pointer' to indicate which block we are using. The pointers are put in at memory locations 2040 to 2047 (Fig. 7.5). We need to use the correct pointer for the level of sprite that we have selected, so for a level 7 sprite we have to use the address 2047. The number that we POKE into this address will represent the location of the block of memory that will be used to store the sprite numbers, and the same reference number will always refer to this set of data. We can choose numbers between 13 and 20. Suppose we choose 13. The next command will therefore be:

POKE 2047,13

and we're almost ready to put the data in place. Since each block of numbers consists of 64 numbers, then the thirteenth block will start at address $64 \times 13 = 832$. Note that this enables us to hold 'spare' sprite data ready for use. We must now poke the data numbers into addresses starting at this figure of 832, and this is done by a FOR ... NEXT loop:

FOR N = 0 TO 62: READ D:POKE 832 + N,D:NEXT

This completes the creation of the sprite, and we next have to think about where we want to have the sprite appear on the screen.

Position and movement

The sprites are positioned and moved on the screen by using a set of number co-ordinates. The X co-ordinate represents positions across the screen, like TAB numbers. The Y co-ordinate represents positions *down the screen*. The starting place for these sprite co-ordinates is the top left hand corner, the same HOME position at the top left hand corner that we use for printing. The co-ordinate numbers also have a greater range than TAB numbers. For printing, we use 40 character positions across the screen and 25 lines down. For sprites, we use up to 320 points across the screen and up to 200 points down the screen. The location point for a sprite is taken as being its top left-hand corner, so that if we use co-ordinates X = $\emptyset$ and Y = $\emptyset$, then we will place the sprite so that its bottom left-hand corner is at the top left hand corner of the screen. Note that the bottom left hand corner of the sprite is not necessarily the first block that is filled in, it is the first square at the bottom left hand corner of the set of 24 by 21, whether it is filled in or not.

The position of each sprite is dealt with by poking its proposed X and Y co-ordinates into a separate set of memory addresses. For a level 7 sprite, we use address VC + 14 for the X co-ordinate, and VC + 15 for the Y co-ordinate. VC, you remember, is the Video Chip address of 53248. To make a sprite appear and move, we have to POKE numbers into these addresses and then change these numbers. Putting numbers in causes the sprite to appear and changing the numbers causes it to move. We do not have to rub out the old image when we use a new sprite position – this is done automatically so that sprite animation is made much easier than animation by other methods.

Suppose, then, that we want our caravan to move across the screen from left to right, and to appear about halfway up the screen. Our Y range is up to 200, so if we use a Y co-ordinate of $1\emptyset\emptyset$, the caravan should appear with its wheels somewhere near the middle of the screen. Remember that it will be the top left-hand corner of the entire sprite which will appear at the co-ordinate points. All we have to do to achieve the correct Y co-ordinate entry is to POKE VC + 15,$1\emptyset\emptyset$. The X co-ordinate is not quite so simple. We want the sprite to move all the way across the screen, calling for a range of $\emptyset$ to $32\emptyset$ for the X co-ordinate, if the caravan is to disappear from the right hand side of the screen. The maximum size of number that we can poke into a memory, however, is 255, so that for the higher values of X, a constant must be added. This is done by poking a number into the address VC + 16. For a level 7 sprite, this number will be 128, so that the instruction is:

POKE VC + 16, 128

This has the effect of adding 256 to the X co-ordinate number, so that the movement from left to right has to take place in two steps:

FOR X = ∅ TO 255: POKE VC + 14, X:NEXT
POKE VC + 16, 128: FOR X = ∅ TO 64: POKE VC + 14, X:
  NEXT
POKE VC + 16, ∅: REM RESET

Since we can have up to eight sprites operating at the same time, we need eight pairs of memory addresses to hold their X and Y co-ordinates. These memory addresses are shown in Fig. 7.6. The extra position that is needed, called the MSB (meaning Most Significant Bit) to get X values from 256 to 32∅ is stored at VC + 16 as we have seen. The program of Fig. 7.7 illustrates these changes so far.

Starting Address for Video Chip = 53248
Using VC = 53248, we can indicate X and Y co-ordinate numbers as VC + n, where n is a number up to 16

Value of n	*Use*
∅	X co-ordinate for Sprite ∅
1	Y co-ordinate for Sprite ∅
2	X co-ordinate for Sprite 1
3	Y co-ordinate for Sprite 1
4	X co-ordinate for Sprite 2
5	Y co-ordinate for Sprite 2
6	X co-ordinate for Sprite 3
7	Y co-ordinate for Sprite 3
8	X co-ordinate for Sprite 4
9	Y co-ordinate for Sprite 4
1∅	X co-ordinate for Sprite 5
11	Y co-ordinate for Sprite 5
12	X co-ordinate for Sprite 6
13	Y co-ordinate for Sprite 6
14	X co-ordinate for Sprite 7
15	Y co-ordinate for Sprite 7
16	MSB store

Fig. 7.6. The sprite X and Y co-ordinate addresses.

The control over sprite position that can be obtained using the POKE addresses for X and Y co-ordinates extends well beyond simple movement. We can double the size of any sprite in either the X-direction, the Y-direction, or both. This is done by poking to addresses VC + 23 (to expand Y) and VC + 29 (to expand X). The numbers that are poked to these addresses will have to be the sprite

```
10 VC=53248
15 PRINT"♥"
20 POKE VC+21,128
30 POKE 2047,13
40 FOR N=0TO62:READ D:POKE 832+N,D:NEXT
50 POKE VC+15,100
60 FORX=0TO255:POKE VC+14,X:FOR J=1TO25:NEXT:
NEXT
70 POKE VC+16,128:FORX=0TO64:POKE VC+14,X:FOR
J=1TO25:NEXT:NEXT
80 POKE VC+16,0:POKEVC+21,0:REM RESET
100 DATA0,0,0,0,0,0,0,0,0,0,2,0
110 DATA2,63,192
120 DATA7,255,252
130 DATA31,255,252
140 DATA63,255,254
150 DATA49,255,254
160 DATA49,255,142
170 DATA127,255,254
180 DATA127,227,254
190 DATA127,227,254
200 DATA127,227,254
210 DATA63,227,254
220 DATA63,227,248
230 DATA28,0,112
240 DATA28,0,112
250 DATA1,182,0
260 DATA1,36,0
280 DATA1,182,0
```

Fig. 7.7. The complete sprite program so far.

level numbers (1,2,4,8,16,32,64 or 128). Try adding this line:

45 POKE VC + 23, 128: POKE VC + 29, 128

to see the effect of doubling the size of this sprite. The size on a 14″ screen is now about 35 mm by 25 mm, about one tenth of screen dimensions.

Multiple sprites

We can create more than one sprite at a time, and these additional sprites can be of different shapes, of the same shape, and of the same shape but different size. Since we have placed all the data to form our caravan shape into block 13 of memory already, we can use it to add more sprites of the same shape. How do we do this? If we make the new sprite at level 6, then the number that has to be poked is 64, and the sprite is turned on by using address VC + 21. If we want to retain our original sprite, however, we need to *add* the numbers that are poked to this address. Since 128 + 64 = 192, then line 2∅ has to be altered so as to read:

2∅ POKE VC + 21, 192

We then have to provide the location of data for this sprite. Since its level is 6, the data block 13 that we have filled has to be poked to address 2∅46 rather than to 2∅47 this time, so we add in line 3∅:

POKE 2∅46, 13

to make the line now read:

3∅ POKE 2∅47, 13: POKE 2∅46, 13

None of this will make the new sprite appear, however, because we have not yet put values of X and Y co-ordinates into its position registers. Suppose we make the Y-position somewhere near the bottom of the screen by using

55 POKE VC + 13, 18∅

Since the range of values in the Y direction is up to 200, 180 should represent a position reasonably near the bottom of the screen. We now have to add the X co-ordinate by having:

POKE VC + 12, X

at around the same part of the program as we have VC + 14 in the original version. We also have to change the MSB of 128 in line 7∅ to 192 to accommodate the new sprite, and the program is now ready to run, as Fig. 7.8 shows.

We can now demonstrate the priority of sprites. If we shift the Y position of the level 7 sprite to 16∅ by a change in line 5∅:

POKE VC + 15, 16∅

and then put its X co-ordinate to halfway along the screen by:

POKE VC + 14, 16∅

then we can keep it there by removing the changes in X co-ordinates in lines 6∅ and 7∅, leaving only the movement of the level 6 sprite.

```
10 VC=53248
15 PRINT"⊐"
20 POKE VC+21,192
30 POKE 2047,13:POKE2046,13
40 FOR N=0TO62:READ D:POKE832+N,D:NEXT
45 POKEVC+23,128:POKEVC+29,128:REM EXPAND
50 POKE VC+15,100
55 POKE VC+13,180
60 FORX=0TO255:POKE VC+14,X:POKEVC+12,X:FOR J=
1TO25:NEXT:NEXT
70 POKE VC+16,192:FORX=0TO64:POKE VC+14,X:POKE
VC+12,X:FOR J=1TO25:NEXT:NEXT
80 POKE VC+16,0:POKEVC+21,0:REM RESET
100 DATA0,0,0,0,0,0,0,0,0,0,2,0
110 DATA2,63,192
120 DATA7,255,252
130 DATA31,255,252
140 DATA63,255,254
150 DATA49,255,254
160 DATA49,255,142
170 DATA127,255,254
180 DATA127,227,254
190 DATA127,227,254
200 DATA127,227,254
210 DATA63,227,254
220 DATA63,227,248
230 DATA28,0,112
240 DATA28,0,112
250 DATA1,182,0
260 DATA1,36,0
280 DATA1,182,0
```

Fig. 7.8. Introducing a second sprite of the same shape.

The new program is shown in Fig. 7.9. When you run this, it shows the level 6 sprite (small caravan) passing in front of the level 7 sprite (large caravan). Just for good measure, we've added a sales message!

Now by changing the priorities, we can make the large caravan into a level 5 sprite (requiring a 32 to be poked in place of 128) in lines 2∅ on:

```
2∅ POKE VC + 21, 96
30 POKE 2∅45, 13: POKE 2∅46, 13
45 POKE VC + 23, 32: POKE VC + 29, 32
5∅ POKE VC + 11, 16∅
56 POKE VC + 1∅, 16∅
```

```
10 VC=53248
15 PRINT"⬛"
17 PRINT:PRINT"CARAVANS BIG OR SMALL,WE SUPPLY
THEM ALL"
20 POKE VC+21,192
30 POKE 2047,13:POKE2046,13
40 FOR N=0TO62:READ D:POKE832+N,D:NEXT
45 POKEVC+23,128:POKEVC+29,128:REM EXPAND
50 POKE VC+15,160
55 POKE VC+13,180
56 POKEVC+14,160
60 FORX=0TO255:POKEVC+12,X:FOR J=1TO25:NEXT:NEXT
70 POKE VC+16,64:FORX=0TO64:POKEVC+12,X:FOR J=
1TO25:NEXT:NEXT
80 POKE VC+16,0:POKEVC+21,0:REM RESET
100 DATA0,0,0,0,0,0,0,0,0,0,0,2,0
110 DATA2,63,192
120 DATA7,255,252
130 DATA31,255,252
140 DATA63,255,254
150 DATA49,255,254
160 DATA49,255,142
170 DATA127,255,254
180 DATA127,227,254
190 DATA127,227,254
200 DATA127,227,254
210 DATA63,227,254
220 DATA63,227,248
230 DATA28,0,112
240 DATA28,0,112
250 DATA1,182,0
260 DATA1,36,0
280 DATA1,182,0
```

Fig. 7.9. A stationary sprite and a moving sprite.

This establishes a new level 5 sprite – the large caravan – and we can see what happens by running the program. The results are disappointing! The large caravan does not appear! The small caravan appears, and at the middle of its journey, it seems to be shadowed. The reason is that our level 5 sprite is sitting at the correct position, but it is invisible because it happens to be the same colour as the background.

The cure is to change the colour of the sprite. When we first create

```
10 VC=53248
15 PRINT"⧉"
17 PRINT:PRINT"CARAVANS BIG OR SMALL,WE SUPPLY
THEM ALL"
20 POKE VC+21,96
30 POKE 2045,13:POKE2046,13
40 FOR N=0TO62:READ D:POKE832+N,D:NEXT
45 POKEVC+23,32:POKEVC+29,32:REM EXPAND
50 POKE VC+11,160
55 POKE VC+13,180
56 POKEVC+10,160
57 POKEVC+44,5
60 FORX=0TO255:POKEVC+12,X:FOR J=1TO25:NEXT:NEXT
70 POKE VC+16,64:FORX=0TO64:POKEVC+12,X:FOR J=
1TO25:NEXT:NEXT
80 POKE VC+16,0:POKEVC+21,0:REM RESET
100 DATA0,0,0,0,0,0,0,0,0,0,2,0
110 DATA2,63,192
120 DATA7,255,252
130 DATA31,255,252
140 DATA63,255,254
150 DATA49,255,254
160 DATA49,255,142
170 DATA127,255,254
180 DATA127,227,254
190 DATA127,227,254
200 DATA127,227,254
210 DATA63,227,254
220 DATA63,227,248
230 DATA28,0,112
240 DATA28,0,112
250 DATA1,182,0
260 DATA1,36,0
280 DATA1,182,0
```

Fig. 7.10. Priority levels illustrated.

sprites, the colours are set in colour registers VC + 32 to VC + 46. Of these, VC + 32 to VC + 36 deal with background, but VC + 39 to VC + 46 deal with sprite colours. We can change the colour of a level 5 sprite by poking to address VC + 44, and by using POKE VC + 44, 5 we get a sprite which is green. The complete program, Fig. 7.10, shows the small caravan passing behind the large one, showing that the level 5 sprite has priority over the level 6 one. Figure 7.11 shows

Value	Colour	Value	Colour
Ø	Black	8	Orange
1	White	9	Brown
2	Red	10	Light Red
3	Cyan	11	Grey (1)
4	Purple	12	Grey (2)
5	Green	13	Light Green
6	Blue	14	Light Blue
7	Yellow	15	Grey (3)

Fig. 7.11. Colour code numbers for sprites.

the colour codes which can be poked into the registers to create sprites of different colours.

Sprite collisions

The register system allows us to check for 'collisions' of sprites. A collision occurs when any part of one sprite touches any part of another, and such events are detected by the sprite-sprite collision register at VC + 30. If we are using levels 5 and 6, then the register numbers of 32 and 64 add to give 96, so that this is the number that will appear in the collision register (which normally contains zero) when these levels of sprites touch. By adding lines 65 and 66 to the program, having deleted the word NEXT in line 6Ø, we can try this – Fig. 7.12 shows the complete program. The PEEK action reads the contents of the register as the sprite moves, and in this example, stops the program when a collision is detected. There is a rich choice of possibilities here – you could print a message, reverse the direction of the small caravan, start the large one moving, or whatever you like. The register at VC + 31 can be used in a similar way to detect when a sprite is touching the background colour.

A further refinement is to allow the sprite to have lower priority than text. Normally a sprite appears 'in front' of text on the screen, but by poking a sprite level number into register VC + 27, this priority can be reversed. In this way, is is possible to have some sprites appearing in front of text and some behind.

Another remarkable set of sprite experiments can be carried out with sprite levels Ø and 1. These can be multicolour sprites, as the program in Fig. 7.13 shows. The multicolour sprite select register is at VC + 28, and by poking 1 into this register, we make a level Ø

```
10 VC=53248
15 PRINT"⊃"
17 PRINT:PRINT"CARAVANS BIG OR SMALL,WE SUPPLY
THEM ALL"
20 POKE VC+21,96
30 POKE 2045,13:POKE2046,13
40 FOR N=0TO62:READ D:POKE832+N,D:NEXT
45 POKEVC+23,32:POKEVC+29,32:REM EXPAND
50 POKE VC+11,160
55 POKE VC+13,180
56 POKEVC+10,160
57 POKEVC+44,5
60 FORX=0TO255:POKEVC+12,X:FOR J=1TO25:NEXT
65 IF PEEK(VC+30)=96 THEN STOP
66 NEXT
70 POKE VC+16,64:FORX=0TO64:POKEVC+12,X:FOR J=
1TO25:NEXT:NEXT
80 POKE VC+16,0:POKEVC+21,0:REM RESET
100 DATA0,0,0,0,0,0,0,0,0,0,2,0
110 DATA2,63,192
120 DATA7,255,252
130 DATA31,255,252
140 DATA63,255,254
150 DATA49,255,254
160 DATA49,255,142
170 DATA127,255,254
180 DATA127,227,254
190 DATA127,227,254
200 DATA127,227,254
210 DATA63,227,254
220 DATA63,227,248
230 DATA28,0,112
240 DATA28,0,112
250 DATA1,182,0
260 DATA1,36,0
280 DATA1,182,0
```

Fig. 7.12. Detecting sprite-sprite collisions.

sprite into a multicoloured one with different colours at 'openings'
and at edges. Colour changes can be made by poking numbers into
VC + 37 – the variety is limitless!

```
5 VC=53248
10 POKEVC+21,1:REM SPRITE 0
20 POKE2040,13
30 FORN=0TO62:READ D:POKE832+N,D:NEXT
40 POKEVC,160:POKEVC+1,100
41 POKEVC+23,1:POKEVC+29,1
42 POKEVC+28,1
43 POKEVC+37,5
45 STOP
80 POKE VC+16,0:POKEVC+21,0:REM RESET
100 DATA0,0,0,0,0,0,0,0,0,0,2,0
110 DATA2,63,192
120 DATA7,255,252
130 DATA31,255,252
140 DATA63,255,254
150 DATA49,255,254
160 DATA49,255,142
170 DATA127,255,254
180 DATA127,227,254
190 DATA127,227,254
200 DATA127,227,254
210 DATA63,227,254
220 DATA63,227,248
230 DATA28,0,112
240 DATA28,0,112
250 DATA1,182,0
260 DATA1,36,0
280 DATA1,182,0
```

Fig. 7.13. Multicolour sprites (level $\emptyset$ and 1 only).

Colour displays

Like graphics characters themselves, colours can be added from the
keyboard or as POKE instructions to addresses in the memory of the
computer. Colour is most effective when it is used in large areas,
because when a colour TV is used for display, the displayed colours
are usually poorly focussed and positioned. This is the fault of TV
design rather than of the computer, and good quality colour pictures
can be obtained from a colour monitor such as the type which can be
used with video cassette recorders. We shall assume for the purposes
of this chapter, however, that only a normal colour TV is available.

The colours which are printed on the number keys will cause text or graphics to appear in colour if these keys are pressed at the same time as the control key [CTRL]. If, for example, you press [CTRL] and 8, you will thereafter get yellow characters appearing on a colour TV screen. You will generally find that the tuning of the TV receiver is much more critical for colour signals than for B/W, so that a good test is to set up a colour signal on the screen. Draw a yellow + sign at each corner of the screen and one in the middle. 'Draw' means type in this case, because the + is a keyboard character. Adjust the tuning of the receiver as described in Chapter One so that each cross appears clear, and then adjust the colour controls until the colour intensity looks about right. To check for colour balance, add some red and blue + signs, and try to balance the control settings so that they all look about equally bright. This adjustment can be very time consuming, because small alterations can often have a considerable effect, but once correctly set up, the receiver should stay that way for a long time. If a colour monitor is being used, of course, the only controls will be intensity, brightness and contrast.

In addition to the eight colours (including black and white), that

Keys	Colour
CTRL+	
1	Black
2	White
3	Red
4	Cyan
5	Purple
6	Green
7	Blue
8	Yellow
C= +	
1	Orange
2	Brown
3	Light Red
4	Grey ⎫ different shades
5	Grey ⎭
6	Light green
7	Light blue
8	Grey (third shade)

Fig. 7.14. The colour codes that are obtained from the keyboard.

◊ PRINT"[CTRL3]RED[SPC][CTRL6]GREEN[SPC][CTRL8]YELLOW"

Fig. 7.15. Colours obtainable within PRINT instructions by using key codes.

can be attained by using [CTRL] with the number keys, another set of colours (see Fig. 7.14) can be obtained when the Commodore key (**C**) is held down along with a number key.

Colour effects can be obtained within programs by using the colour keys within PRINT instructions. Figure. 7.15 shows an example of a text line printed in different colours – the program is written using the C.T. standards to indicate the control key pressed. A print-out of this program would not reveal which key had been pressed, so that this method of writing is necessary for programs that make use of these special keys.

Another method of putting colour into text, which can, of course, include graphics strings, is to make use of the colour code numbers which are shown in Fig. 7.16. These numbers are used along with the CHR$ instruction, as the program in Fig. 7.17 illustrates. The advantage of this method is that the program can use CHR$(CL) (for example) to control the colour, with the number variable CL being set to different values so as to obtain different colours. We could, for example, use a READ ... DATA to obtain different values of CL at different stages in the program. Note how the use of blue characters makes the READY prompt invisible.

POKE colours

By using POKE instructions, we can alter the colour of the border

Colour	CHR$ *Number*
White	5
Red	28
Green	3◊
Blue	31
Black	144
Purple	156
Yellow	158
Cyan	159

Fig. 7.16. Colour codes for use with CHR$.

```
10 PRINT CHR$(158)"YELLOW"
20 PRINTCHR$(30)"GREEN"
30 PRINTCHR$(156)"PURPLE"
40 PRINTCHR$(31)
```

Fig. 7.17. Using the CHR$ colour codes.

and the background of the screen in addition to the colour of the text. The addresses that we have to use are the video chip addresses 53280, which controls border colour, and 53281, which controls background colour. The values which can be poked into these addresses were illustrated in Fig. 7.11. Any value up to 255 can, in fact, be poked into these addresses, but only the listed values will affect the colour.

When we use the POKE instruction to place graphics or text characters directly on to the screen, we can also POKE colours to the same positions. The colour memory (Fig. 7.18) for the screen extends from address 55296 to address 56295 (1000 places in all), and these numbers correspond exactly with the addresses for the screen positions. For example, POKE 1024, 105 will place a block on to the top left hand corner of the screen, and POKE 55296, 7 will change the colour of that block to yellow. Since there is a one-to-one correspondence between the position numbers and the colour memory numbers, we can use instructions like:

DF = 54272
POKE PO, DA: POKE PO + DF,CL

In this example, the variable DF is the number difference between the colour POKE address and the position POKE address. If we use variable PO for a position address and DA for a character number, then POKE PO, DA will place the data (character) in place. With CL used for the colour code, then, POKE PO + DF, CL will put the colour code into the correct memory to affect the character. The colour numbers that must be allocated to CL are picked from the same range of 0 to 15 as were illustrated in Fig. 7.11.

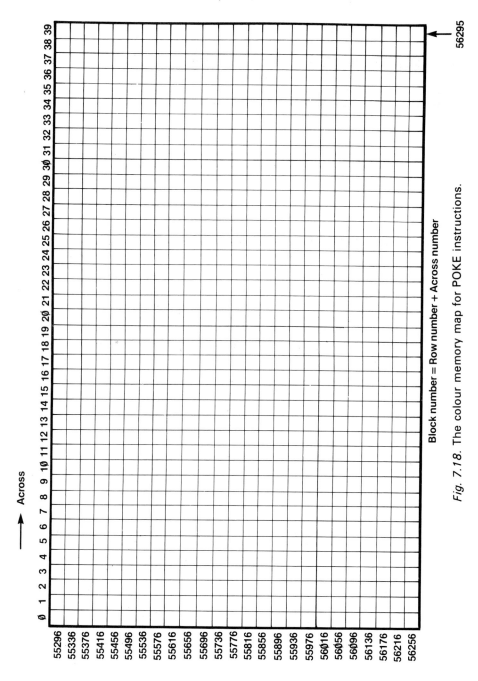

Block number = Row number + Across number

Fig. 7.18. The colour memory map for POKE instructions.

Chapter Eight
Function Keys and the Sound Generator

Function keys

Many new designs of computers feature 'user-programmable keys' which can easily be programmed, using BASIC, to carry out an action or even a series of actions initiated by pressing one key. The function keys of the Commodore 64, however, are not simply programmable in this way. They can be used in a BASIC program as a way of responding to questions on the screen (PRESS f1 for YES, f3 FOR NO), because each key has a corresponding code number (see Fig. 8.1). For really effective use, however, these keys have to be

Key	CHR$ number
f1	133
f2	137
f3	134
f4	138
f5	135
f6	139
f7	136
f8	140

Fig. 8.1. The CHR$ codes for the function keys.

programmed using machine code, which is outside the scope of this book. This is why the manual for the 64 makes practically no reference to these keys. Programs available for the 64 in cartridge form make very effective use of the function keys, however.

The sound generator

A sound generator is virtually essential for any computer that is to be used for games programs. Its inclusion in a machine which is also an excellent choice for business use can be justified by the additional scope that this gives. Several operations in data processing programs take a noticeable time to perform, particularly string sorting, so that it is useful if the operator does not have to concentrate on screen messages while such processes continue. The use of sound as a prompt allows the operator more freedom in this respect, and the use of different notes for different types of advice is a distinct help to the user. The sound generator of the 64 is considerably more advanced than is needed just for these purposes and it allows many of the actions of a simple music synthesiser to be carried out. The sound channel does not use an internal loudspeaker because the tiny loudspeaker which would be needed could not do justice to the sound. Instead, the sound signal can be taken from the audio/visual socket at the rear of the case. This output can be connected to a hi-fi or other sound system to allow the sound to be played or recorded. Alternatively if a TV receiver is in use rather than a monitor, the TV volume control can be used to control the sound level at the loudspeaker of the TV. In this case no additional connections are needed – the sound signal is sent to the TV receiver along with the vision signal. Whichever method is used, the user can control the volume of sound externally, which is a most desirable feature!

Musical notes

Though it is easy to learn to program the sound generator of the 64, full benefit of the system can be obtained only if you have some understanding of sound. A musical note consists of vibrations in the air, and the number of vibrations per second is called the frequency (Fig. 8.2). Our ears detect this as the pitch of the note, so that a note whose frequency is 100 vibrations per second (called 100 hertz) sounds low to our ears, a bass note. A note whose frequency is 3000 vibrations per second (3 kilohertz) sounds high to our ears, a treble note. The sensation of pitch can therefore be expressed by a number, the frequency of the sound vibrations.

The volume of a note is measured by the amount or amplitude of the vibration, and the sound generator of the 64 is represented by a scale of $\emptyset$ (no sound) to 15 (maximum volume). The maximum setting should be used until you have some experience of the sound generator, because you can independently control the sound volume

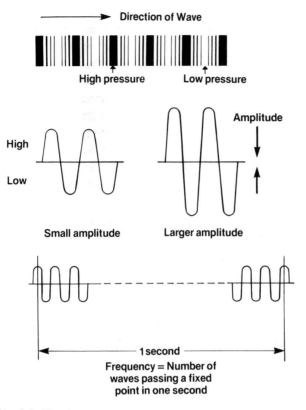

Fig. 8.2. The frequency and amplitude of a sound wave.

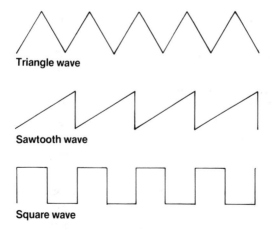

Fig. 8.3. The waveforms that the 64 can generate.

at the TV receiver or hi-fi unit in any case. Control of volume by the 64 is used to alter the volume of one note relative to another, rather than to set the volume of a complete sound program.

Your ear can readily distinguish between the same pitch of note played on different instruments, and this is because of the different waveshapes or waveforms. The waveshape (waveform) is the appearance of the graph of amplitude of vibration plotted against time for one complete vibration, and the types of waveform that the 64 can generate are shown in Fig. 8.3. These are four basic types of waveshapes, but a musical note can be much more complicated than this, because a note may consist of several waves of different amplitudes (Fig. 8.4). Instruments which make use of hammers

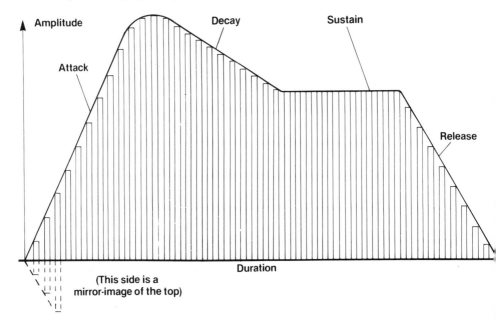

Fig. 8.4. The 'envelope' of a set of waves. Changing the envelope shape has a very considerable effect on the sound.

(piano, drums) have a sharp 'attack', meaning that the vibrations rise to a large amplitude very rapidly and die away more slowly. The dampers of a piano can also ensure that a note can die away (decay) rapidly after a short time, so that the 'envelope' shape has attack-sustain-decay and release sections. These separate sections can be programmed, so that the type of sound can be varied as well as the pitch, volume and waveform.

In addition, the 64 has three 'voice' settings, meaning that up to three notes can be sounded simultaneously. This has obvious applications in generating music, but the use of pleasant chords to announce the end of a process and discords to announce errors can be very useful in data processing work as a reminder to the operator. We'll spend the rest of this chapter on programs which allow you to explore some of the possibilities of the sound generating system of the 64. Before starting, though, you should be certain that you have read and understood the section on binary numbers in Chapter Seven, and the use of POKE in Chapter Six.

The sound POKEs

To produce a sound, the following POKE instructions have to be carried out:

1. Volume, using address 54296.
2. Waveform, using a different address for each voice.
3. Attack/Decay, using a different address for each voice.
4. Sustain/Release, using a different address for each voice (optional).
5. Frequency, using the two addresses 54273, 54272.

In addition, a FOR ... NEXT loop has to be set up to control the time for which each note is played, and the note has to be cancelled by further POKE instructions so that it will not repeat on the next FOR ... NEXT loop.

Assuming that we leave volume set at maximum for our first experiments in sound, what do we have to use to create a sound? The next item on the list is waveform, of which the 64 provides four choices. A simple constant volume sine wave sounds like a whistle, and is a sound that the ear soon tires of. The musical instrument that comes nearest to this waveshape is the flute, and a human whistler can produce sine waves which when displayed on a cathode-ray oscilloscope (which can show waveform shapes on a TV-like screen)

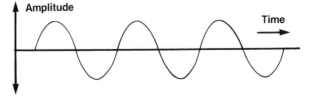

Fig. 8.5. A sine wave, the simplest waveform of all. Other waveform shapes can be analysed into a mixture of sine waves of different frequencies.

look almost perfect (Fig. 8.5). Because the pure sine wave is used to such a small extent in music (and because it's difficult to generate!), the 64 uses the choices of triangle, sawtooth, square and noise signals.

The triangular wave produces interesting sounds, and is programmed by the code number 17. The three voices of the 64 use three different addresses for poking this waveform code number; they are 54276 for voice 1, 54288 for voice 2, and 54290 for voice 3. Figure 8.6 shows a program that will produce notes which have a

```
10 PRINT"PRESS ANY KEY TO START"
20 GET K$:IF K$=""THEN20
30 POKE 54296,15:REM VOLUME
40 READ AD:IF AD=0 THEN END
50 POKE54277,AD
55 PRINT"ATTACK/DECAY NUMBER IS ";AD
60 POKE54276,17
70 POKE 54273,34:POKE 54272,75:REM NOTE
80 FORT=1TO250:NEXT
90 POKE54276,0:POKE 54273,0:POKE 54272,0
100 GOTO20
200 DATA128,129,130,132,136,64,65,66,68,72,32,
33,34,36,40,16,17,18,20,24,0
```

Fig. 8.6. The effects of different attack/decay values on a triangular waveform.

triangular waveform, using the same pitch and volume settings but with different combinations of attack and decay. The attack starts with the maximum setting and with zero decay, and the decay rate is raised in four steps, following which the next level of attack is used. There are twenty notes played in all, and you can hear for yourself how the different attack and decay rates affect the character of the notes that are produced. This program deliberately uses notes of long duration so that you have time to hear the effect of each change. In normal use, we would have timing loop values of closer to 100 to 200 rather than the 250 that is used in this program.

In addition to the values shown in the program, however, we can add the attack and decay numbers so as to obtain a whole new range of effects. If we consider the attack/decay address as a set of eight bits (Fig.8.7) then the attack is controlled by the top four bits and the decay by the bottom four. In this way, numbers ranging from 255 (maximum attack and decay) down to 16 (lowest attack, no decay)

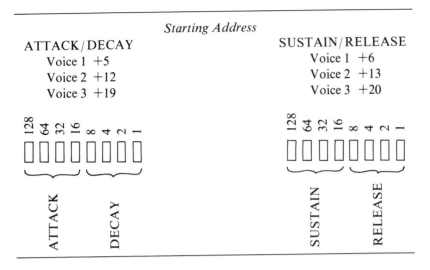

Fig. 8.7. Analysing the attack/decay numbers.

can be used. This gives a very large range of possible effects to experiment with, but you have to remember that you can't just change numbers in a simple add-one, subtract-one way. Figure 8.8 shows a chart that helps to unravel the two separate sections of the attack/decay number so that you can choose your separate values of attack and decay and then combine them into the correct number to poke into memory. The same methods can be used for the sustain/release numbers.

Now try the same program of Fig. 8.6 with line 6Ø changed so as to use the sawtooth waveform by poking 33 in place of 17. The notes this time appear to be quite different, although the pitch is the same. Try also the square wave, obtained by poking 65, and then the noise (poke 129) in new versions of line 6Ø to appreciate the wide range of sound effects that can be created by this very versatile system. Figure 8.9 shows a summary of the design of sound programs.

Warning notes

The program of Fig. 8.10 gives a sharp buzz which is useful as a warning note. This can be used as a reminder that an incorrect key has been pressed, or that an incorrect command has been issued or incorrect option taken in a program. The buzz program is written as a subroutine which would be called by an IF ... THEN test

ATTACK/DECAY		SUSTAIN/RELEASE

Attack Section   *Sustain Section*

Value	Time
0	2 ms
1	8 ms
2	16 ms
3	24 ms
4	38 ms
5	56 ms
6	68 ms
7	80 ms
8	100 ms
9	250 ms
10	500 ms
11	800 ms
12	1 s
13	3 s
14	5 s
15	8 s

Decay Section   *Release Section*

Value	Time
0	6 ms
1	24 ms
2	48 ms
3	72 ms
4	114 ms
5	168 ms
6	204 ms
7	240 ms
8	300 ms
9	750 ms
10	1.2 s
11	2.4 s
12	3.0 s
13	9.0 s
14	15 s
15	24 s

Combining times:
ATTACK/DECAY Select attack number, multiply it by 16, and add decay number.
SUSTAIN/RELEASE Select sustain number, multiply it by 16, and add release number.

Note: Times are ms (milliseconds, equal to thousandths of a second) and s (seconds).

Fig. 8.8. How to combine attack/decay (and sustain/release) numbers.

(1) Set volume by poking to 54296. The same number is used no matter which voice is selected.

(2) Set Attack/Decay level. This needs a poke to a different register for each voice. The Attack/Decay should be poked before the waveform is set – if you don't do this, the volume level may seem disappointingly low.

(3) Set Sustain/Release. This is optional, and you can omit it.

(4) Poke the note numbers – two addresses for each voice.

(5) Set the waveform – one address per voice. The settings of 17 and 33 are the most useful for the musical notes. 129 is useful for noise effects. The pulse wave, 65, is not particularly useful unless you can find more information on its use. When the pulse waveform is selected, a different pair of addresses have to be poked with note values.

(6) Put in a timing loop to set the duration of the note. Values of 250 or so are useful. If you select a very long wait, the note may die away too much. If you select a very short time, the note may never get beyond its attack stage.

(7) Turn off the waveform, attack/decay and sustain/release settings. If you do not, the note will continue after the program has ended.

Fig. 8.9. Sound program design summarised.

somewhere in the main program or in another subroutine, such as:

```
500 GET A$
510 IF A$ = "W1" THEN GOSUB 10000
520 PRINT "DO YOU REALLY WANT TO WIPE THIS
    FILE?"
530 (continue routine ...)
```

Variations on this theme can be used to signal different conditions. For example, the buzz can signify an incorrect entry, and two buzzes, or a longer buzz with a different pitch, can signify a

```
10 GOSUB10000
20 END
10000 VL=54296:WF=54276:AD=54277:NH=54273:NL=
54272
10030 POKEVL,15:POKEWF,33:POKEAD,15:POKENH,34:
POKENL,75
10040 FORN=1TO100:NEXT
10050 POKENL,0:POKENH,0:POKEAD,0
10060 RETURN
```

Fig. 8.10. A warning-note program.

serious error, like destroying data if you proceed. A musical note (try a triangular wave with small attack and decay numbers) can signal that the program needs attention, but not urgently. This might be used to draw attention to the need for entry of information. Note that in the program of Fig. 8.10 the poke addresses have been assigned to variables that should remind you of their uses. This greatly simplifies the use of sound in programs. A further simplification is made by using standard subroutines, such as that shown in Fig. 8.11, though generally it is better to make the initial settings

```
10 VL=54296:WF=54276:AD=54277:NH=54273:NL=54272
20 POKE VL,15
90 GOSUB 11000:GOSUB 12000
100 INPUT"NUMBER";A
110 IF A>10THEN GOSUB 11030:GOSUB13000:PRINT
"MUST BE LESS THAN 11":GOTO100
120 END
11000 REM SET UP VOICE 1
11010 POKE WF,33:POKE AD,15
11020 RETURN
11030 REM SET UP SOUND 2
11040 POKE WF,17:POKE AD,65
11050 RETURN
12000 REM NOTE 1
12010 POKE NH,34:POKE NL,75
12020 FOR TM=1TO250:NEXT:POKE NH,0:POKE NL,0
12030 RETURN
13000 REM NOTE 2
13005 FORN=0TO50
13010 POKE VL,N:POKENH,34:POKENL,100
13020 NEXT
13025 POKENH,0:POKENL,0:POKEAD,0
13030 RETURN
```

Fig. 8.11. A typical set of sound subroutines illustrated.

of volume, waveform, attack/decay and possibly sustain/release at the start of the main program – this could alternatively be done in another subroutine which concentrates on all set-up conditions. Each sound subroutine can then make use of these initial settings. Another possibility is to have a set of several subroutines which allow a choice of sound settings. In this way, the appropriate subroutine is called before the sound is needed so that the correct poke instructions have been carried out in advance, and only the frequency value has to be set. The example shows the two simple notes used in contrasting warnings – one to advise that an input is expected, the other to warn that the input is unacceptable.

Sound subroutines

Having introduced the subject of sound subroutines, a few more useful subroutines can now be examined. These are grouped as set-up routines and note routines, because of the fact that it is often more useful to keep the two separate. For many uses, a single set-up routine, or two at most, may be sufficient.

Figure 8.12 shows a subroutine which produces a warbling note.

```
1∅ VL=54296:WF=54276:AD=54272:HF = 54273:L
F=54272
2∅ POKEVL,15
3∅ POKEAD,19∅
4∅ POKEHF,17:POKELF,33
5∅ POKEWF,17
7∅ FORW=1TO25∅:POKEHF,19:FORJ=1TO1∅:
NEXT:POKEHF,17
8∅ NEXT
9∅ POKEWF,∅:POKEAD,∅
1∅∅ END
```

Fig. 8.12. A subroutine to produce a warbling note.

This is a note routine only, as it can be used along with any of the set-up routines. A warbling note is a better attention-getter than a steady note, though the effect should not be overdone. Note that it is possible to make each note continue until a key is pressed by incorporating the GET A$ instruction into the sound loop. This can be more useful to force attention than sounding a single note which may be unheard or ignored.

The note routines that we have used up to now have made use of a time delay loop to get the time of the note. Any loop will act as a time delay, and a loop which pokes gradually changing values into the volume setting address will cause the volume of the note to change during the time while the note is being sounded. This can cause interesting effects, as illustrated in Fig. 8.13. If the volume was originally set by means of a separate set-up routine, it is advisable to

```
1Ø VL=54296:WF=54276:AD= 54277:HF=54273:L
F=54272
2Ø POKEAD,19Ø
3Ø POKEHF,17:POKELF,33
4Ø POKEWF,17
5Ø FORN=1TO15STEP.1
6Ø POKEVL,N
7Ø NEXT
8Ø POKEWF,Ø:POKEAD,Ø
1ØØ END
```

Fig. 8.13. Changing volume settings within a note.

store the original value at the start of the subroutine (using another variable) and then restore the value at the end of the subroutine, so that the next subroutine that uses the sound settings will be able to start with the volume correctly set.

The delay loop can also be replaced by a loop which changes the pitch of the note within a FOR ... NEXT loop. This produces rising or falling notes which can be used as games sound effects or for attention-getting in business programs.

Chapter Nine
Sorting Out and Other Topics

The Commodore 64 is such a versatile computer that it's difficult to find space within one book to explain some of the instructions when they can't be naturally associated with a group. This chapter is therefore dedicated to the forgotten actions in the belief that some of them will turn out to be very useful to you in your own programs.

One of these is FRE(X). X can be any number variable, even if no value has ever been assigned to X. It's called a 'dummy variable' and the only reason for its presence is that it's easier to have a useless variable in an instruction than to design the computer to cope with an instruction that has no variable following it. FRE always has to follow something else like PRINT or MEM = , and what it provides is the number of unused bytes in the memory. This can be extremely useful if you are using a data program which places a lot of data into the memory, because you can use FRE to print a warning:

> IF FRE(MM) = 5∅ THEN PRINT"NEARLY OUT OF
> MEMORY":PRINT"PLEASE RECORD DATA NOW.":
> GOTO   (or GOSUB)

and then start a recording to dump the data before the program is brought to an untimely end by an OUT OF MEMORY message

Another instruction in this miscellaneous group is SGN(X). The variable name that is used here is not a dummy this time, it must be a number variable, and the value of SGN(X) will indicate the sign of the number represented by X. If, for example, we have:

> SG = SGN(NR)

then SG will be +1 if the number NR is positive, −1 if NR is negative, and ∅ if NR is zero. A line such as:

> IF SGN(NR) =−1 THEN PRINT "NEGATIVE VALUE":
> GOTO ...

can be used to avoid a hang up due to, for example, trying to take a square root of a negative number. If you don't need such a warning, simply a change of any negative values to positive ones, then ABS(NR) will give the positive value of any number. By using NR = ABS(NR), we eliminate any negative quantities that might have been allocated to the variable NR. To change the sign of a number (+ to − , − to +), we can write:

NR = NR *—1

Debugging commands

Every now and again, a new program works almost as we expected it to. Much more frequently, it doesn't, and we have to investigate to find out why. In computer parlance, the program has a bug in it, and we have to debug it. What title we create for ourselves in carrying out this work I leave up to your imagination. If we wrote the program in the form of a core with subroutines, as advised in Chapter Five, then sorting out what part of it is causing trouble should be comparatively easy. Once you know where a program has failed, then it seldom takes long to find the causes, except when the machine uses a complicated version of BASIC. You will find that the BASIC of the 64 is particularly simple to work with when things go wrong, and the commands STOP and CONT will help you considerably in debugging.

STOP means what it suggests. If you place the STOP command in a program anywhere, in a line by itself, or as one statement in a multi-statement line, then the program will stop at that point. What is more valuable is that everything remains intact. All of your program variables retain the values that they had when the program stopped so that you can check any values by a direct command like:

PRINT TL, SM, PR, NM$

to see that has happened to your variables. This facility exists until you type RUN, or until you edit or enter a new line. If you have not changed the program in any way, then typing CONT (for continue) and then pressing RETURN will allow the program to carry on from where it left off.

How can we make use of this? There are two ways, since STOP can be executed by having a program line containing the word, or by pressing the STOP key when a program is running. The use of the

STOP key is particularly useful if a program seems to have got itself into a long loop and is showing no signs of emerging under its own steam. Pressing the STOP key will stop the program, and the message BREAK IN ... will come up on the screen, specifying the line that was being executed when the program was stopped. You can then take a close look at your program, listing lines and printing variable values, to see what the reason for the problem might be. Some string-sort routines can take a remarkably long time, and a good way of deciding whether the delay is natural or not is to print the values of all the quantities that change during the sorting process, or in whatever loop appears to be giving trouble. Note these values (write them down, don't trust to memory!), type CONT and press RETURN to start the program again, and then use the STOP key again some time later. When you print out the variables again, you ought to see some changes in the right direction. If not, then the loop is faulty in some way, and the chances are that it will never finish correctly. The values that you have noted, however, should provide you with some clue as to why the loop has stuck.

The STOP that is inserted into a program line, or in a line of its own, is particularly useful when you have an idea of where the fault might be, but the program runs too fast for you to be able to pinpoint the place where the trouble starts. The program may, for example, use several subroutines before it gets into difficulties. A STOP placed just before the RETURN part of a subroutine will allow you to find, by printing variable values, what the subroutine has done. If all is well, you can type CONT, press the RETURN key, and you will find the program stopping at the end of the next subroutine ready to inspect another set of variables. You can place as many STOP instructions as you like in a program, but remember that you will have to take them out again when you have found the fault.

END can be used to ensure that a program does not 'crash-through' into a subroutine accidentally. When the program comes to and END, you will not get any BREAK IN ... message, simply the normal cursor appearing on the screen. If there is another section of program, or even a different program, following the END, then CONT will allow this to run. If, however, you use CONT at the genuine END of the program, on the highest numbered line, then you will get a CAN'T CONTINUE error message. You will also get this message if you try to use CONT when the program has stopped due to an error.

CONT and STOP are such useful devices for debugging that it is hard to believe that not all computers use them both. Even one rather expensive and much-praised machine totally lacks the CONT command, making debugging a long and difficult business, even if all the bugs are only in the user's program!

Program testing

Program debugging and program testing go hand-in-hand, but testing can start seriously only when all of the bugs that I class as 'silly-but-serious' have been eliminated. A silly-but-serious bug in this sense is one like a syntax error which will cause the program to hang up displaying an error message. There is, on the other hand, no harm in starting to test a program which has a few faulty print commands, such as printing badly divided or with the data poorly displayed, since these will not cause any hang-ups. Any fault which can cause an error message must be dealt with, however, because if you need to input a lot of data to test a program then there's a chance that all your effort will be lost if the program stops and you aren't careful about preserving the data. If the program stops with an error message, then you cannot use CONT to pick up the threads again. If you use RUN, then all of your variables will be reset and you will lose all of your data. You may be able to continue by picking a line number at which you can restart (a good one to pick is usually the start of the menu), and then using GOTO line number, press RETURN, to get a second chance. This, on the other hand may simply lead you to the same fault again, or to another one.

A method that I use for large data handling programs is always to test in sections as the program is being developed, and to ensure that the core program has a "DUMP DATA TO TAPE" option, even if this is not needed in the program. Provided that the dump routine is reliable, this allows me to use GOTO with the line number of the start of the menu, and to dump all of the data on tape (or, of course, disk) if anything untoward happens. Since 90% of the time that is needed for testing a data processing program can be in the entry of data, this hint can save many hours of work.

In general, testing is a thoroughly boring, frustrating and utterly essential piece of drudgery. At every INPUT or GET part of the program, you will have to try each possible incorrect response. These must either be rejected, if the error can be detected (like a number in place of a letter or a number in the wrong range), or questioned, such as:

ARE YOU SURE? (Y OR N)

If the program works with numbers, try it on numbers that are very near to the limits of acceptability – very small and very large. Generally, if a program works with the extremes, it should work with everything in between, but watch out for zero! A divide-by-zero error is always one that will hang the program up with the error message. The other point to watch is that you do not suffer from cumulative errors caused by the way that the computer stores numbers in binary form. If you always remove excessive decimal places before comparing numbers, then this should present no problems.

If the program works with strings, then try very short strings and very long strings, strings that start with upper-case (capital) letters, strings that start with lower-case (small) letters, similar-looking strings, strings containing numbers and all the other evil entries that can appear. In particular, always remember to test what happens when RETURN is pressed without having pressed any other key. This should result in a blank string that the computer can deal with, but in some cases it can cause problems, particularly when LEN is used, and string slicing takes place. If the program uses arrays, check that the dimensioning cannot be accidentally exceeded. One fruitful cause of this can be when a set of results are printed in neat columns using two loops of the style:

FOR N = 1 TO 3∅∅: FOR J = ∅ TO 3
PRINTTAB(1∅*J); L$(N + J): NEXTJ: PRINT: NEXT N

This looks innocent enough, but when the dimensioning of L$(N) has been for 3∅1 items, you will get an error message in the last line. When N = 3∅∅, as it must when the N loop is almost ended, the J loop will force the computer to find items L$(3∅∅) to L$(3∅3), even if there are no entries in the array beyond 3∅∅. This is harmless enough, but if the dimensioning was only for 3∅1 items, then 3∅2 cannot be accepted. A good way of testing for dimensioning errors is to test the program with the dimensionings deliberately low – you can use 5, for example, over-riding the normal 10 that is allowed. This makes testing to the limits much easier.

If the program contains a string sort, ensure that the dimensioning is adequate, and that the entry of items will be automatically aborted if any attempt is made to add an item beyond the dimensioned limit. Some programs cope well with initial entry, but permit items to be added later on with no warnings that they may be taking the total number beyond limits. A crash during a sort may leave some of your data in a peculiar state, to say the least. Any string sort should always be tested with the maximum number of items, and this is something that you cannot simulate by using small numbers. One method is to add temporarily to the program a subroutine (Fig. 9.1)

```
5 DIMS$(100)
6 S$=""
10 FORN=1TO100
20 FORJ=1TOINT(RND(1)*8)
25 G=INT(RND(1)*26+65)
30 S$=S$+CHR$(G)
40 NEXT
50 S$(N)=S$
55 S$=""
60 NEXT
```

Fig. 9.1. Creating random 'words' for testing programs.

that generates the correct number of 'words' made out of letters chosen at random, and with random length (perhaps from two characters to nine). You may then find that a string sort which is perfectly satisfactory for 50 entries is desperately slow for 350 entries. It's better to find this out at the testing stage than later when you are sorting a set of strings that took you the best part of a couple of days to enter. Even if nothing can be done to speed up the sort (and something can *always* be done) then it's a comfort to know that it will finish eventually, rather than leave you wondering if the computer is in an endless loop. Just for the record, a string sort that I once used (never again) took 1½ hours.

Patience is the name of the testing game, and the ultimate test is to write brief instructions, and have someone who has had no part in designing the program test it for you, with no prompting. It can be a humiliating experience, but it will certainly teach you a lot about testing!

Machine code access

When you type an instruction word like PRINT in BASIC, this causes a long chain of actions to start. These actions are carried out by the microprocessor (a type 6510) inside the 64, and its instructions are in the form of electrical signals. We can convert these electrical signals to and from binary number codes which don't mean very much to you unless you have had a lot of experience with them. Programs written in these number codes are called machine code (or object code) programs.

In the space of a book that is dedicated to the 64 and its programming in BASIC, we can't possibly start to deal with the writing and use of machine code, but we can deal very briefly with the ways in which the 64 can make use of such programs. Machine code can be placed in the memory from cassettes, from disks, or by means of cartridges, and each machine code program will have some unique starting address in the memory. This address has to be passed to the computer – it may be stated in the program documentation. To make the machine code program run, you will then need one of two instructions SYS or USR, unless a cartridge is being used. Cartridges are normally self-starting, and need no special action on your part.

The simpler of the two start-up commands is SYS (SYStem). Typing SYS followed by an address number in denary will, when you press RETURN, have the effect of starting the microprocessor executing machine code that starts at that address. Machine code is executed very quickly so that unless the program causes some noticeable effect, like printing a message on the screen, you may not be aware that the program has run. The SYS command is used when the machine code is a 'patch', meaning a piece of code that adds some modification to the behaviour of the machine itself, rather than one which operates on the values of variables that are present in a BASIC program. A typical 'patch' might be one which added a new command word "DUMP" which sent any picture on the screen to the printer to be reproduced.

When variables are operated on by a machine code program, then the instruction USR(X) is used in preference to SYS. The address at which the machine code starts is placed in coded form into two memory locations, and the variable X has a value that will be used by the machine code program. When the machine code has done its work, a new value may be passed back, as for example by use of a line such as:

$$NX = USR(X)$$

in which the value NX is one that has been obtained by the action of the machine code on the quantity X.

The real-time clock

The 64 reserves two variable names, TI and TI$, for maintaining a 'real-time clock'. The phrase 'real-time' is used to distinguish the action of timing in seconds from the action of the high-speed 'clock' pulses which determine the speed at which actions are carried out.

The variable TI is used as a counter. When the computer is switched on at first, TI is reset to zero, and its value is incremented (increased by 1) at intervals of 1/100 second (Europe) or 1/120 second (US and Japan). The limit to the count is 16,777,215 – this means that the value of TI will let you time more than 46 hours (European version) before the value resets. TI$ is a more useful time display, consisting of hours, minutes and seconds. When TI$ is reset, using TI$="∅∅∅∅∅∅", then TI is reset also. Note the quotes round the zero, made necessary because TI$ is a *string* variable, not a number.

TI can be used in delay loops which must be exactly timed – for example:

```
1∅∅ S = TI
11∅ IF TI < S + 1∅∅∅ THEN 11∅
12∅ PRINT "END"
```

which gives a ten-second delay (in Europe). For a ten second delay in the US, use 12∅∅ in place of 1∅∅∅ in line 11∅.

TI$ can be used to establish a time display that can be called up at any stage in a program. An outline for this is shown in Fig. 9.2 in the

```
10 PRINT"⊐":ST$=""
20 PRINT:PRINT
30 PRINT"PLEASE TYPE HOUR - USE 24 HOUR CLOCK";
40 INPUT H$:IF LEN(H$)=1 THEN H$="0"+H$
50 PRINT"PLEASE TYPE MINUTES";
60 INPUT M$:IF LEN(M$)=1 THEN M$="0"+M$
70 PRINT"..NOW SECONDS..";
80 INPUT S$:IF LEN(S$)=1 THEN S$="0"+S$
90 IF LEN(H$+M$+S$)>6 THEN PRINT"MISTAKE -
PLEASE TRY AGAIN":GOTO10
100 TI$=H$+M$+S$
110 PRINT"⊐":PRINT:PRINT:PRINT
120 PRINT"TIME IS ";LEFT$(TI$,2)+":"+MID$
(TI$,3,2)+":"+RIGHT$(TI$,2)
130 S$=RIGHT$(TI$,2)
140 IF RIGHT$(TI$,2)=S$THEN140
150 GOTO110
```

Fig. 9.2. A digital clock program using TI$.

form of a digital clock program. Lines 1∅ to 9∅ establish values of hours, minutes and seconds in string form. If any value is a single figure, it is then padded out with a zero so as to conform to the standard that is needed for TI$. Finally in line 1∅∅, TI$ is equated to the string of hours, minutes and seconds. From this point on, TI$ will be synchronised to the time of day, so that printing TI$ will produce a time display. This is not in a very readable form, however, and line 12∅ improves on it by adding colons between each of the three separate sections of TI$. In addition, if TI$ is updated in a loop, the screen will flicker very noticeably, so that lines 13∅,14∅ ensure that the loop caused by the GOTO11∅ in line 15∅ is traversed only as each second is completed. This is done by using a temporary variable S$ to hold each value of seconds, and keeping the program looping in line 14∅ while TI$ contains the same value of seconds.

In a program, the time value might be set initially, using lines 1∅ to 1∅∅, but the value might be printed as a reminder only at intervals (perhaps each 20 minutes), not using the continuous loop that has been illustrated. Line 12∅ is, however, a useful method of displaying the time which can be used in other subroutines. Alternatives to display include sending a warning when a preset time is reached (alarm clock action), recording a time on cassettes of data, or printing a time on memos.

Chapter Ten
System Expansion and Advanced Features

Printer connection

The 64 allows for the connection of the Commodore printer to the serial port. The serial port is one from which data is taken piece by piece in sequence, and this port permits inputs or outputs. Only the Commodore printer can be connected directly – the use of any other type of printer requires modifications either to software (adding a 'driver' program) or to hardware (adding an interface). A particular advantage of using the Commodore printer is that it will reproduce on paper the effects that appear on the screen.

The use of a printer is essential for most data processing purposes, and business users may feel that they need two printers, one dot-matrix type for fast printing which need not be of the highest quality, and one daisy-wheel type which is slower, but which gives print quality comparable with a good electric typewriter. At the time of writing, ink-jet printers which combine reasonable prices with fairly high quality were just becoming available. Your local Commodore dealer will be able to show you examples of work printed on different types of printer. The 64 will permit more than one printer to be connected at the same time, selecting which one is used by the OPEN statement, assuming that suitable interfaces are used.

Communicating with other computers

The 64 is constructed so that it can be used in networks with other 64 machines. By using the serial input/output connections, data can be fed into or out from the computer. The source or destination of the data can be another computer, and the system can be arranged so that one computer can control the other. The serial input/output can be used along with a device called a modem to send and receive computer signals over the telephone lines, allowing your 64 to pass data to or receive data from any other 64, and possibly other machines as well. This facility is useful if the telephone system permits links of reasonable quality, but if the service is poor, then radio links may be preferable. In some countries, pigeon post is quicker!

Joysticks, paddles, graphics tablets and light-pens

Joysticks and paddles are traditionally associated with games, but can also find uses in data processing applications. The use of a joystick, for example, can allow the computer to be operated by a partially disabled person, providing that the programs have been written with this in mind. Joysticks can also be useful in point-of-sales applications, in which the customers can use the joystick to move an arrow on the screen to select an item of information. This is usually preferable to allowing the keyboard to be used, because the joystick use can be controlled by the program in such a way that no fatal mistakes can ever be made. By contrast, the use of the keyboard, with its inviting STOP and BREAK keys, can soon result in a program crash, which does not inspire confidence.

Graphics tablets, as the name suggests, are like miniature drawing boards. A drawing traced on the graphics tablet can cause a corresponding pattern to appear on the screen of the computer, and a suitable program will allow the data from the drawing to be recorded and later replayed. The matching accessory, the XY plotter, will produce a drawing from X,Y co-ordinates and on/off pen controls fed to it from the computer, and is a very valuable accessory when the computer is used in drawing offices. The prices of graphics tablets and XY plotters have been traditionally very high, as these were normally used only with high-priced computers, but the falling price of computers has caused a fall in the price of these accessories. The fall has not assumed great proportions as yet, but we can expect that in the near future you will not have to pay more for a graphics tablet or an XY plotter than for any other computer accessory, and certainly not as much as the computer cost.

The light-pen is, as its name suggests, a pen-like object whose tip is light-sensitive. The light-pen is connected to the computer and used to detect light, usually on the screen, under the command of a program. One typical use is in drawing patterns. When the tip of the light-pen is placed close to the screen, a spot of light appears on the screen where the light-pen is pointing, and this remains lit when the pen moves on. If the pen is held close to the screen as it is moved, the tip will leave a path of light drawn on the screen. If the pen is lifted away from the screen, drawing stops, but will resume at any other place where you put the tip of the pen against the screen.

The light-pen requires both hardware (the pen and its cable) and software. For a drawing program, the software consists of a routine which pokes each screen address until the light-pen responds. The points which do not cause any response are restored to their original contents, but when the point that causes a response is found, the character poked into this address is allowed to remain. This is repeated as the pen moves, but the search is easier when the pen is kept in contact with the screen, because only the area round the point of contact needs to be searched. This search program needs to be written in machine-code, because BASIC is generally too slow to respond.

The light-pen can also be used in menu selection, pointing to an item that you want to select, or for deleting an entry (draw a line across the item with the light-pen). These uses are particularly appropriate for business purposes, in which the light-pen can often provide an alternative to typing an entry. This has obvious advantages for many disabled users, and also the advantage that the keyboard need not be made available to all users of the program.

Cartridge options

The 64 provides for a range of plug-in cartridges which contain memory that is already programmed in a permanent form. This can be used to add new facilities to the machine in a particularly simple way. The IEE-488 cartridge, for example, allows the 64 to make use of the attachments which were designed for the older CBM designs, notably the PET series. If you already have a PET printer or disk system, for example, or have developed control equipment that is operated by a PET, then the 64 with its IEE-488 cartridge will also connect to and operate the same equipment.

A PET Emulator cartridge is also available which allows the 64 to run programs that were designed for the PET computer. This allows you access to a huge range of well-tried and well-known software, and, once again, allows you to replace a retired PET with a 64 without having to replace all of the valuable software.

The Z-80 cartridge contains more than just a program in memory.

It contains a Z-80 type of microprocessor, and by re-allocating the memory of the 64 and controlling it with the Z-80, this allows the CP/M operating system to be used on the 64. This can be good news if you have a considerable investment in CP/M programs which can be transferred from another machine into the 64, but the system is not quite so attractive as it might appear. Programs that use CP/M will generally be on disk, and it is unlikely that a disk created by a different type of machine will be able to operate on the 64 disk system. This is why the method of passing the program from one machine to the other is more useful. In addition, it would be pointless to use the CP/M option just to gain access to software, because the price of CP/M software is very high. Several CP/M programs cost more than the 64 itself, and in general you could obtain programs to carry out the same results much more cheaply if you do not use CP/M but concentrate on the PET option. In addition, CP/M was designed to be used by professional programmers rather than users, and is not particularly easy or convenient compared to some other systems, particularly if you have only the manuals to go on.

Another cartridge option is Simons BASIC. This consists of a very greatly extended BASIC language that contains a large number of the instructions that have appeared in other versions of BASIC. It offers a choice of new keywords which greatly extend the usefulness of BASIC, and in particular allows graphics and sound programming to be carried out much more easily without the use of POKE instructions. The use of this BASIC, however, eats up a very large part of the memory of the 64.

The use of cartridges can permit other programming languages to replace the BASIC of the 64, and also permits the BASIC to be replaced by specialist programs. Other languages, such as PASCAL, very popular among academics, and FORTH, used for machine-control, can be achieved with cartridges, and machine code programs, such as word-processor programs, can replace BASIC, so as to leave a lot of free memory available for text. All of these cartridges will eventually be available from your Commodore dealers – and probably sooner than I shall be able to get a working operating system for my other computer!

Disk systems

A disk system is virtually essential for a computer that is to be used for business purposes. A disk drive consists of mechanical parts which can grip a thin plastic disk and revolve it at 300 r.p.m. A record/replay head can then be positioned over tracks in the disk, and data can be recorded on to the magnetic coating of the disk, or replayed if the disk has previously been recorded. Included in the same casing as the disk drive, however, must also be a disk controller. An important difference between a disk system and the use of a cassette recorder is that the disk system is operated under complete computer control. Any disk command that is contained in a program will cause the disk to be spun at the correct speed, the head to be placed on the correct track, and the correct data read, or new data recorded in the correct place. All that the user needs to do is to ensure that the correct disk is in place! All of this, however, needs a very complex control system, which is the factor that accounts more than anything else for the price of disk systems.

The control system for Commodore disk system uses its own complete computer system and memory built into the disk system itself. Because of this, disk systems made by other manufacturers are not generally suitable for Commodore systems, since most of these other systems make use of the computer in some way. The Commodore system has the great advantage that the addition of a disk system to the 64 does not require any of the memory of the computer. Many other types of computers use 3K to 5K of the computer's own memory in order to control the disk system, and in some cases this leaves very little room for programs in the computer.

Other developments

At the time of writing, several miniature disk systems, using disks ranging in diameter from 3" to 4", are on the point of production. These systems are in no way inferior to 5¼" disks in terms of storage, and we can expect the use of such miniature disks to increase if only the manufacturers can agree to a common standard. At present, each disk system for 5¼" disks uses different standards, so that disks are not interchangeable, even when a common operating system such as CP/M is used. If a common standard for smaller disks can be agreed, then the advantages to software suppliers will be enormous. If there is no agreement, we can expect to find the same conditions applying to the miniature disks as to 5¼" disks, and there will be little, if any, incentive to use the smaller disks. At present, the only agreement is on the format of the older type of 8" disk, but 8" disk drives are less common on the smaller computers.

These and other newly developed devices will be evaluated for use on your 64, and put on sale whenever Commodore are convinced of their usefulness. Keep a close watch on the computing magazines, and on the local Commodore dealers to keep in touch with progress.

Last word

We've reached the end of this particular path now. With the formalities of introduction now complete, you and your 64 now have to get thoroughly acquainted. You can do this by tackling problems, not the problem examples that you find in some textbooks, but your own real problems. It's by using the 64 for problem solving on your own applications that you will make the most rapid steps in learning the art of program design and the rather lower level craft of using BASIC to carry out that design. Happy programming!

Appendix

The BASIC of the Commodore 64 is MICROSOFT, which is regarded as a worldwide standard form of BASIC, and is very widely used on computers. Two computers, however, use instructions which differ considerably from MICROSOFT in some details. These are the Acorn Atom, whose BASIC is very different from MICROSOFT, and the Sinclair ZX series, in which a different instruction is used for the LEFT$, MID$ and RIGHT$ of MICROSOFT. The table below deals with the conversions which are needed for programs written for these computers so that these instructions can be used.

XZ Series	Commodore
LET B$ = A$(3)	B$ = MID$(A$,3,1)
LET B$ = A$(TO 3)	B$ = LEFT$(A$,3)
LET B$ = A$(3 TO)	B$ = RIGHT$(A$,5) assuming LEN(AS) = 7
LET B$ = A$(3 TO 5)	B$ = MID$(A$,3,3)

Atom	Commodore
$B = $A $B + 3 = ""	B$ = LEFT$(A$,3)
$B = $A + 2	B$ = RIGHT$(A$,2)
$B = $A $B + 6 = "" $B = $B + 2	B$ = MID$(A$,2,6)

Index